Unintended Consequences

Or "Why Do Bad Things Happen To Good Decisions?"

Unintended Consequences

Or "Why Do Bad Things Happen To Good Decisions?"

Clive Wills

IFF
BOOKS

Winchester, UK
Washington, USA

JOHN HUNT PUBLISHING

First published by iff Books, 2020
iff Books is an imprint of John Hunt Publishing Ltd., No. 3 East Street, Alresford,
Hampshire SO24 9EE, UK
office@jhpbooks.com
www.johnhuntpublishing.com
www.iff-books.com

For distributor details and how to order please visit the 'Ordering' section on our website.

Text copyright: Clive Wills 2019

ISBN: 978 1 78904 288 7
978 1 78904 289 4 (ebook)
Library of Congress Control Number: 2019941538

A CIP catalogue record for this book is available from the British Library.

Design: Stuart Davies

UK: Printed and bound by CPI Group (UK) Ltd, Croydon, CR0 4YY
US: Printed and bound by Thomson-Shore, 7300 West Joy Road, Dexter, MI 48130

We operate a distinctive and ethical publishing philosophy in
all areas of our business, from our global network of authors to
production and worldwide distribution.

Contents

For my brother Dixe Wills, for his encouragement way beyond the call of duty and for never once suggesting that I might be treading on his toes.

This world runs on unintended consequences. No matter how noble your intentions, there's a good chance that in solving one problem, you'll screw something else up.[1]
– Rand Beers, member of the US National Security Council

There are unintended consequences to everything.[2]
– Steve Jobs, co-founder of Apple

Introduction

This book was sparked into being by a deeply frustrating experience. I had embarked on what I imagined would be a brief and routine correspondence with HMRC, the UK tax authority. All I needed was to have a form stamped by the local office. However, the matter proved to be more complex than I had anticipated. They would only communicate by post, and so letters began passing back and forth between us. The matter was rather urgent, but it seemed to take ages for me to get a response. So I sent them follow-up letters in an effort to hurry things along. Mysteriously, when I received replies, the letters were dated two weeks earlier, even though the tax office was only a mile away from me in central London. In the end, I became so exasperated that I arranged to go to their office to meet with my correspondent, and she stamped the form for me on the spot. In response to my query about the time lag in our correspondence, she revealed that it was caused by a new and "more efficient" internal postal system. In order to save money on postage costs, outgoing letters were being rerouted via a central hub in Nottingham, but the new system was so unwieldy that it took a fortnight for mail to work its way through it. As a result, correspondence was crossing in the post, so that staff were having to deal with the same request on multiple occasions. Thus, whilst a few pence per letter were saved on postage costs, this was completely eclipsed by the unintended consequence of the extra workload caused to staff by the inefficiency of the system, to say nothing of the frustration and delays suffered by myself and their many other communicants.

Shortly after that, on an occasion that is still painful in the remembrance, the boot was on the other foot. I, an experienced London Underground traveller, was on my way to work when I was asked by a foreign-speaking tourist for assistance in reaching her destination. She was going to Euston Station, which was on my route, and so I helpfully accompanied her to ensure that she reached it safely. However, once we had arrived, she very carefully explained to me that she had actually just come from Euston, so that I had in fact taken her back to the station which she had started from some 30 minutes earlier.

I then came across another instance where good intentions simply weren't enough. It was in an episode of *The Simpsons*, in which the home of Ned Flanders had been demolished by a hurricane. However, because of their love for Ned, his neighbours rallied round and quickly rebuilt it for him. As they all had their own ideas of the design it should have, it had a somewhat unusual, even geometrically impossible look. Once it was completed, Homer Simpson asked him, "So, Ned, what do you think of the house that love built?", but before Ned could respond, the entire edifice collapsed due to the shoddy workmanship and lack of any coherent design. Marge commiserated with Ned, and observed that, "We meant well, and everyone here tried their best," to which Ned's bitter response was, "Well, my family and I can't live in good intentions," and he sarcastically observed that, "We can't blame you, because you had 'Good Intentions'." Ned and his neighbours had discovered that, no matter how much love someone may have, good intentions aren't always enough.[3]

In 2017 the charity Oxfam ran a campaign to highlight the fact that the richest 85 people in the world controlled as much wealth as the 3.5 *billion* poorest. Whilst building houses may be beyond us, many of us will feel that we can help people out by moving money from the comparatively rich (i.e. us) to the poor. But here too dangers lurk. Jon Kuhrt, who managed a cold weather shelter in Soho in central London, wrote that the location gave the residents a base that they could use to develop their skills in begging and shoplifting. They used the duvets that the hostel provided to give the impression that they were sleeping rough, so that concerned tourists would give them money. However, the cash then went straight into the hands of Soho's many crack and heroin dealers. As one of the homeless observed when asked to take part in an activity in the hostel, "I'll tell you what – if you get members of the public to walk through the hostel lounge and drop fivers and pound coins in my lap – then I'll stay in."[4] A straightforward transfer of money from rich to poor may not always be for the best, although there are other ways to help. There is a range of organisations which exist to help rough sleepers in the UK, such as Crisis, Centrepoint and St Mungo's. Rough sleepers can also be referred to an operation called Streetlink,[5] which puts the homeless in touch with the most appropriate agency. So, if you have a concern for the homeless, why not set up a regular donation to, or do some work with, an appropriate charity?

Unintended consequences can ruin even the most trivial of acts. A train driver pithily wrote to a newspaper that he had, "Just killed a bird at Birchgrove Station because someone put bread down for them on the platform."[6]

Our use of words can be just as problematic as our actions. Dr George Thompson, President of the splendidly named Verbal Judo Institute, advises police forces on their use of language, pointing out that it is only too easy to say something which will have exactly the opposite effect. For example, telling someone to "Calm down!" tends to be seen as being critical of their behaviour and will only give them another reason to be upset. Similarly, ordering someone to "Come here!" just warns them that they are in trouble and that they should probably scarper as quickly as possible.[7]

We all have goals that we would like to achieve in life. Like HMRC, we may wish to save a bit of money or, like Homer Simpson, we may want to help a neighbour. From the trivial to the life-changing, we will be faced with challenges on a daily basis. Whether consciously or otherwise, we will adopt a course of action that we believe will enable us to achieve those ends.

Whilst we may succeed, there will be many occasions when we need to adopt a more subtle approach.

A common problem provides a typical example. In the middle of the night, an increasingly exasperated parent is doing their very best to get an unsettled baby to sleep. Their judgement being somewhat fuddled by their own lack of sleep, they try a number of different methods. They pick the infant up, rocking her back and forth, and when that has no immediate effect they lay her down and wind up her mobile, which plays gentle music as it turns. As the baby is still awake, they begin to read a story. Of course, in the clear light of day we can see that the baby is becoming more and more overstimulated and will never get to sleep with all that activity going on, but at the time, with the best of intentions, the poor parent is failing in the one thing that they most wanted to achieve. As Tim Lott, an exasperated father, observed, "The real problem is that most children don't want to go to sleep when you tell them to... Going in and shouting 'Go to sleep!' is not an effective solution. I should know, I've tried enough times."[8]

And I suspect that many of us have a single friend who, despite being very nice and personable, has become so desperate in their attempts to find a partner that they either fling themselves at the most unsuitable people or are so obvious in their attempts to attract a mate that they merely frighten off the source of their affection.

And sometimes there are extremely straightforward cases, such as the elderly Buddhist lady who, just before boarding her flight from Shanghai Airport, threw nine coins into the plane's engine as a way of praying for safety.[9] Fortunately, airline staff were alerted by concerned fellow passengers. Eight of the coins missed, but one landed inside the engine. The flight eventually left five hours late once the coin had been retrieved.

By taking a deep breath and thinking these problems through rationally, with perhaps a little external advice, we should be able to plot a course of action which will bring about the required result. Sometimes it is as simple as not throwing coins into a plane's engine, but unintended consequences can be cunning things, and by their very nature will often take us by surprise. It is hoped that this book will, by examining a wide range of unintended consequences across all aspects of life, help us to become more aware of their dangers and provide some tools to enable us to avoid them and achieve what we set out to do.

Taking a long-term view is an important start, and is vital not only when parenting and forming relationships, but also in dealing with major national issues such as education and health. However, one major problem with the democratic process is that it tends to encourage (and often almost requires) that governments seek short-term answers to long-term problems. If they fail to do so within their relatively brief time in power, they run the risk of being replaced by an alternative party which is likely to attempt different (but still short-term) answers to the same entrenched issues, thus swaying first one way and then the other without achieving anything. Schools, the Health Service and Law Enforcement have all fallen foul of this approach, with teachers, hospital staff and police officers continually struggling to implement and adapt to new regimes, just in time for them to be thrown out in favour of a new "grand plan". Like the parent with the sleepless baby, the chopping and changing may be enough on its own to ensure failure.

These are complex cases where, even if long-term planning is possible, a straightforward solution is much harder to see and may quite easily not exist at all. If there were an obvious way to run a cheap and efficient National Health Service then all parties would surely work together to follow this course. If producing well educated and responsible young people were simply a matter of putting more money into schools, then by now we would have nothing but legions of smart (in all senses of the word) school leavers stepping out into the world. However, as the 2011 riots in Britain showed only too clearly, modern society is a frustratingly complicated mechanism, apparently immune to simple solutions. As writer HL Mencken has put it, "For every complex problem, there is a solution that is simple, neat, and wrong." With that advice ringing in our ears, let us venture into the jungle of what the Germans know as "verschlimmbesserung" (literally, "improvement for the worst"), or unintended consequences to the rest of us.

Chapter 1

"The best-laid plans of mice and men..."

Which of us has not set out on a course of action, armed with the best of intentions, only to find everything seemingly conspiring against us? Part of the problem is that many aspects of life have become so complicated that we cannot be quite sure what the consequences of an unconsidered action might be. If it is bad enough for us as individuals, it is incomparably more difficult for governments, who often face immensely complex situations as well as often being subject to the short-term interests of voters.

My initial introduction to unintended consequences came in an Economics class at school. We looked at a case where the British Government had attempted to improve the British colour print film market. In the 1960s the US company Kodak was the dominant force, and their only real competitor was the much smaller British company Ilford, who had then been in business for over 80 years. Kodak was perceived as the "quality" product, but Ilford made a reasonable living at the budget end of the market. Following a 1966 report by the Monopolies Commission, legislation was introduced to force Kodak to reduce the price of its colour film. However, by removing the price differential between Kodak and Ilford, Ilford was squeezed out and was restricted to making "own brand" film for the likes of Boots the Chemist. Thus, Kodak's one competitor was removed, and the Monopolies Commission, instead of promoting competition, had actually installed Kodak as an effective monopoly.

This is but one tiny example of how a powerful organisation can take a hammer to a problem, only to have it rebound and hit them on the head, but a catastrophic example unfolded in the wake of the terrorist attacks of 11th September 2001. At that time the US Government was understandably eager to take all possible action against terrorist organisations, and was particularly keen to cut off their sources of funding. It consequently introduced the "Patriot Act", which included regulations designed to make money laundering more difficult and thus make it harder for illegal organisations to use the banking system. However, these regulations also made it trickier for legitimate financiers to trade in the US, and so they became more inclined to invest elsewhere. As they withdrew from the US market, demand for the US dollar, and thus its value, fell.

Meanwhile, President George W. Bush needed to borrow heavily (in the region of US$4 trillion [about £3 trillion]) in order to fund his "War on Terror",* and in particular the invasion of Iraq. One of the ways that he raised this money was by issuing so-called "Patriot Bonds", which were essentially Government IOUs which guaranteed a certain return to the purchaser. In order to attract potential investors, the rate of return had to be higher than otherwise available interest rates. So, in order to make the Bonds more attractive, the benchmark US interest rate was steadily reduced, falling from 6.5% in 2000 to 1.25% by November 2002, before bottoming at a record low of 0.25% in 2003. As the interest rate was reduced, demand for the dollar followed suit and thus its value fell further.

Mortgage rates also followed interest rates down, and so buying a home became more affordable and increased the demand for housing. Property prices therefore followed suit, and as they steadily climbed, housing became a bandwagon that people were ever more desperate to jump aboard, either through fear that failing to buy now could mean that the house they wanted might not be affordable next year or just because of the promise of an easy profit.

As the number of new mortgages grew, so did the profits of the banks that supplied them, and so more mortgage suppliers sprang up to cater for the demand. Of course, the number of new house buyers had to run out eventually, but once demand began to drop off, the lenders, being geared up to supply a steady stream of new loans, looked to potential new markets. They targeted people who would not normally have been able to afford a mortgage or who would not have qualified on other grounds, perhaps because they could not provide a deposit or prove their income. The mortgage companies offered special "bargain basement" introductory offers to these potential buyers, and in many instances did not require any independent proof of income. These customers have since become infamous as "sub-prime" borrowers. However, at the time, with house prices continuing to rise, even if the repayments became unsustainable, buyers could either remortgage or just sell the house at a profit. As millions more Americans began to aspire to own their own home, these mortgages seemed to give them a low-risk means of getting their feet on the property ladder. Such was the popularity of these loans that at the height of the market in March 2007, this type of mortgage issued to sub-prime borrowers had an estimated total value of US$1.3 trillion (about £1 trillion).[10] To put such a figure into some sort of context, this is a little more than the annual production of the whole of Mexico.

Even though these lenders were by definition a risky bet, pressure was being put on salesmen to lend as much money as possible, and whilst one might think that they would be concerned about the possibility of their borrowers defaulting on their loans, the mortgage companies believed that they had this eventuality covered. They employed a sophisticated form of insurance called Credit Default Swaps or "CDS". If the borrowers repaid their loans, all well and good, but if they didn't, the mortgage companies could claim on an insurance policy, so there seemed no way that they could lose. The more mortgages they could issue, the more money they would make, regardless of the borrower's ability to repay the loan.

With no apparent risk to either borrower or lender, anyone staying out of the property market looked a bit of a chump.

However, sucked along by the boom in property prices, inflation in the general economy began to rise. So, in order to take some of the heat out of the economy, the US Federal Reserve began to put interest rates back up, increasing them from 0.25% in 2004 to 5.25% by July 2006, a massive twenty-one-fold increase. At the same time, the "easy initial terms" of many mortgages were coming to an end, and the combination of these two factors caused the rates payable on mortgages to soar and many monthly repayments to double.[11] As so many borrowers were only just able to afford the repayments in the first place, mortgage defaults rocketed and huge numbers of homeowners were forced into selling. Under the American system, borrowers who can no longer afford repayments are able to simply hand back the house to the lender and walk away free of any debt. So, once repayments became unaffordable many did just that. Of course, the sudden resulting increase in the number of houses coming back on to the market meant that property prices not only stopped rising, but began to fall precipitously. With mortgage rates high and values falling, the foundations of the boom were wrenched away, so that demand fell even further, creating a vicious circle of ever-increasing supply and reducing demand.

As the US sub-prime mortgage defaults escalated, one bank in particular began to feel the pressure. In its enthusiasm to ride the US mortgage gravy train, Lehman Brothers bank had bought five mortgage lenders, including sub-prime lender BNC Mortgage and Aurora Loan Services, which specialised in loans to borrowers who lacked proof of income. In 2006 alone Lehman's various companies financed US$146 billion (about £112 billion) in mortgages. Whilst having hundreds of billions of dollars in assets, Lehman also had hundreds of billions of dollars of debts, and as many of its assets could not be speedily turned into cash, it needed a constant inflow of money from other financial institutions to keep its financial engine turning. However, as it became apparent that its mortgage-based assets were losing value fast and becoming all but impossible to sell, the money that oiled the huge machine drained away and on 15th September 2008 it ground to a shuddering halt. With debts of over US$600 billion (about £460 billion) on its books, Lehman Brothers was by far the biggest bankruptcy in US history, bigger than Enron, WorldCom, Chrysler and General Motors combined.

With the fall of Lehman, enormous pressure was placed on the banks and other financial institutions that had lost their money. They accordingly turned to their insurance policies, the Credit Default Swaps, and it quickly became apparent that many of these could be traced back to just one company, American International Group, or AIG, which had written Credit Default Swaps on over US$500 billion (about £385 billion) of assets.

AIG was already suffering similar pressures to Lehman, as it too had invested heavily in the residential mortgage market as well as having over US$400 billion (about £308 billion) in Credit Default Swaps with Lehman. Having allowed Lehman Brothers to go bust, the American Government was now faced with the possibility of a worse disaster, the downfall of AIG, which would in turn have brought down other financial institutions to whom AIG owed money. The American Government had no option but to loan US$180 billion (about £138 billion) to keep AIG afloat.[12]

Lehman's collapse brought about a lethal combination of domino effect and vicious circle and meant that, in order to stop things becoming even worse, governments around the world were forced to bail out banks and insurers, which resulted in many whole countries falling into difficulty. Some, such as Iceland, Greece and Spain, only narrowly averted bankruptcy. Western economies crashed like boulders rolled off a cliff and suffered the worst recession for eighty years.

The cost to US taxpayers of bailout packages and other assistance was the best part of US$10 trillion (about £7.6 trillion)[13] (about 2/3 of the output of the entire US economy in

2008), with European governments contributing a further US$2 trillion (about £1.5 trillion).

Astonishingly, in attempting to defend the West by conducting its "War on Terror", America had initiated a chain of events that, just seven years after the attacks on the World Trade Center, had resulted in the devastation of Western economies – an outcome surely beyond the wildest dreams of any terrorist.

One of the problems for democratic governments is that they so often feel that they ought to be seen to be doing something whenever there is a new outrage or scandal. And if they are to do something, with elections often looming, speed is vital.

The scandal surrounding British MPs' expenses in 2009 was a case in point. An exposé in the *Daily Telegraph* revealed that hundreds of MPs had been abusing the system of paying expenses, including claims for dubious second homes and non-existent mortgages. The more exotic claims included £2,000 (about US$2,600) to repair a leaking water pipe under a tennis court, another £2,000 to clear a moat, hundreds of pounds for horse manure and, most notoriously, Sir Peter Viggers' claim for £1,645 for a "floating duck island" (although that claim may not have been actually paid). 389 current and former MPs were eventually ordered to repay falsely claimed expenses, and within a month of the scandal breaking, 28 MPs had either resigned their cabinet posts, said that they would not stand for re-election or resigned with immediate effect. They included Michael Martin, who became the first Speaker of the House of Commons to be forced to step down in 300 years. Five MPs and two members of the House of Lords were sent to prison for expenses fraud.

As a result, the Government took action to force various types of authorities to make their dealings more transparent. Local councils, for example, had to publish full details of all expenses over £500 (about US$650). Unfortunately, however, putting this kind of information into the public domain has enabled fraudsters to make use of that information to send bogus invoices to the councils in question, masquerading as the genuine suppliers and defrauding the councils.[14] By using this information to convince UK councils to change the bank details of their suppliers, criminals were able to siphon off at least £7 million (about US$9 million) in 2010 alone.[15]

This transparency has also had the effect of revealing the unintended consequences of the Government's money-saving schemes. Thus, when a freeze on recruiting new permanent employees was introduced across Whitehall in May 2010, rather than reduce numbers when staff left, managers instead engaged agency staff at a much higher cost, so that the overall wage bill actually rose by 65% over the following 4 months.[16]

None of this is particularly new. In the 17th century, the British Government introduced a tax which had unintended consequences for the next 150 years. And it all came about because of a problem with coins. If you look at a British £1 or £2 coin, you will see that the edge is milled, and some have a catchy slogan. The ones currently (in 2017) in my pocket have "Standing on the shoulders of giants" round the £2 and "Pleidiol wyf i'm gwlad" ("True am I to my country" for those not conversant in the Welsh tongue) on the £1. However, in the 17th century, there was no such adornment. Many coins at that time were made of silver and thus had a value in themselves. As the coin edges were plain, there was an understandable temptation for the unscrupulous to trim a little off them and thereby gradually accumulate a nice stock of precious metal for themselves. So bad had things become that it was reckoned that by the end of the 17th century the average coin had been reduced to one half of its original weight. The Government therefore wanted to withdraw the coins then in circulation and replace them with brand-new tamper-proof coinage with milled edges. This would be a costly business, and the Government had to find a source of revenue to pay for the new coins. A tax on income was felt to be too controversial, as it would mean that the state would be enquiring into personal matters. (Governments have since become less squeamish.) A "Hearth Tax" at a basic rate of 2 shillings per chimney or stove had been introduced in 1662 but was unpopular as it allowed inspectors to enter each room of a house to count the number of fireplaces. That Act had been repealed in 1689 and was replaced by the grandly named "Act of Making Good the Deficiency of the Clipped Money" in 1696. This was a form of property tax that neither required taxpayers to submit information to the state, nor to have an inspector enter their house. It was reasonably reckoned that the grander a house was, the more windows it would have, and so in 1696 a very simple tax was introduced on windows, with a flat rate of 2 shillings per house and a variable tax for houses with more than 10 windows. Properties with between 10 and 20 windows paid a total of 4 shillings, and those with more than 20 paid a total of 8 shillings. As is so often the way with taxation, the rate steadily increased over the years, being raised six times between 1747 and 1808, by which time the lowest band started at 6 windows and was levied at 8 shillings per window per annum, with a higher rate for houses with more windows.

However, one obvious way of reducing liability for this tax was to have fewer windows in your house, and within 20 years it was noted that the amount being raised from the tax was declining. In 1747, the tax was restructured so that although no tax was paid on houses with fewer than 10 windows, if a house had 10 or more windows a tax of sixpence per year per window was payable on every window. Similar disproportionate increases occurred at 15 and 20 windows. Quite naturally, the result was that builders and house owners tried to ensure that they had the maximum number of windows for the minimum tax, and thus in the mid-1700s nearly 50% of houses had 9, 14 or 19 windows, thereby maximising their tax efficiency.[17] So, when the 34 properties in the Essex village of Woodham Walter were assessed for window tax in May 1761, 11 of them had 9 windows and 5 had 14. None had 10 or 15. When Jane Winn's home in the village was originally assessed, it had 13 windows, but when reassessed four months later these had been reduced to 9, thus reducing the tax from 9½ shillings a year to 3.[18] The property today has become The Bell Inn, and it was only in 1930, when the pub was being renovated, that the blocked up windows were rediscovered and opened up, rectifying 173 years of reduced light and ventilation.[19]

As well as blocking up existing windows, new houses were being built with fewer windows. The theory had been that the tax would just affect the rich, but as it was levied on whole buildings, rather than the individual homes within them, even poor people became liable to pay. Disease and ill health were rife as people in tenements suffered from the gloom and dampness which were exacerbated by the minimal natural light. In 1781, there was a lethal typhoid outbreak in Carlisle. An investigation concluded that the outbreak had begun in a house occupied by six poor families, and that:

In order to reduce the window tax, every window that even poverty could dispense with was built up, and all sources of ventilation were thus removed. The smell in this house was overpowering, and offensive to an unbearable extent. There is no evidence that the fever was imported into this house, but it was propagated from it to other parts of town, and 52 of the inhabitants were killed.[20]

By 1851, with the Industrial Revolution and urbanisation at its peak, new houses were going up everywhere, and yet glass production had not increased at all over a 40-year period. It was then that the unintended consequences finally became too onerous, and the window tax was abolished as income tax took over as the main source of government income. Bizarrely, it is still possible today to see older houses in the UK with blocked up windows – purely as a result of a tax that was done away with over 150 years ago.

Even with today's more sophisticated governments, collecting property taxes is by no means straightforward. As new taxes are introduced, taxpayers are on the lookout for any possible loopholes. All UK property sales must be registered, so it would appear to be an easy task for the Government to collect the stamp duty that it levies on most property sales. However, the very wealthy have found it worth their while to take their property out of UK legislation by placing it in an offshore trust. As the *Sunday Times* reported in January 2012,[21] more than £100 billion (about US$130 billion) of central London property (about 1 in 20 houses) was held in such trusts, thus escaping the clutches of the taxman. The Government, cottoning on to these loopholes, introduced new legislation in the March 2012 budget, placing a punitive 15% tax on properties over £2 million (about US$2.6 million) which were bought by companies. However, increasing complexity inevitably brings a corresponding increase in unintended consequences, so doubtless there will be further developments.

Failing to learn from the British example, in the 19th century New Orleans introduced its own version of the window tax, taxing houses according to the number of storeys. However, only storeys at the front counted for tax purposes, and so, almost inevitably, builders began to construct houses with just one storey at the front, but with more behind, giving rise to the uniquely New Orleans "Camelback" house.[22]

Taxation provides a powerful weapon for governments. As well as raising income, it can also be used to attempt to control people's behaviour, so tobacco and alcohol are often highly taxed. Taxation has existed from time immemorial. The famous Rosetta Stone is a piece of rock that in 196BCE was carved with an important announcement in three different languages – Egyptian hieroglyphs, a written Egyptian script and ancient

Greek, thus providing the key to the translation of hieroglyphs. And what information was so important that it needed to be carved into rock as hard as granite in three different languages? It was to express the thanks of the Egyptian priesthood to the ruler Ptolemy V for having declared a tax amnesty, so taxation had obviously been causing anguish even then. Indeed the Old and New Testaments of the Bible are full of references to taxation. Even in the late 2nd millennium BCE, it seems to have been well established, for we find Joseph telling the Israelites that, "When the crop comes in, give a fifth of it to Pharaoh."[23]

Most taxation is imposed purely to raise revenue, and over the thousands of years since it was first dreamt up, one might imagine that governments would have worked out how to do this efficiently. However, there are many instances in which the instinct to squeeze out more and more from the populace overrides the evidence that increasing tax rates may actually result in reducing the amount raised. Thus, in 1988, UK Capital Gains Tax was increased from 30% to 40%. This is a tax on the profit that has been made on certain assets, but can be avoided easily enough just by not selling those assets. And so it was that such sales fell steadily, decreasing by more than ¾ over the next five years. This far outweighed the increase in tax raised on the sales that did go ahead, resulting in a fall in the amount that this tax collected from more than £2 billion (about US$2.6 billion) in 1987/8 to £606 million (about US$790 million) in 1992/3, a 70% drop. Research indicates that people are very sensitive to this type of tax and that when it is levied at a rate of between 15% and 35%, for every 1 percentage point increase, there is a fall in total income of between 2% and 5%, with the opposite applying if the tax is reduced.[24]

One of the problems with taxation is that it is a blunt instrument, and lays itself wide open to exploitation of its unintended consequences. When VAT was introduced in the UK in 1973, businesses in the Channel Islands (which are not subject to VAT) expressed concern that the time taken to process their flower and dairy exports to the UK (where VAT would be charged) would cause unreasonable delays and that consequently their produce would lose its freshness. Low-cost imports from the Channel Islands were accordingly exempted, and this arrangement worked smoothly for many years. However, by 2011 the VAT rate had risen from its original 8% to 20%, and so, with the advent of Internet shopping, it became worthwhile for Amazon and other online retailers to save the VAT by sending CDs and DVDs from mainland UK to the Channel Islands, before they made the return trip back to the UK customers. Amazon for example sold via their "preferred vendor", a Jersey-based company called Indigo Starfish. Thus, a CD which retailed at £12 from a UK retailer could be sold by Amazon via Jersey at £10 without any reduction in their profit margin. Independent "bricks and mortar" record retailers were already struggling as a result of the fall in CD sales as consumers moved towards downloading music (both legally and illegally) and the price advantage obtained by online retailers was the final straw for many. As a result, between 2006 and 2011 over 2/3 of UK record shops closed (including my local independent store), leaving just 270 in the whole of the country. Graham Jones, author of *Last Shop Standing*, a book about the demise of record shops, said, "Although there are many reasons why stores have closed down, the VAT loophole is by far the biggest contributing factor." As the cost of setting up an operation in the Channel Islands is at least £30,000 (about US$39,000), the small independent shop stood no chance.[25] The larger bricks and mortar retailers were not exempt either, with the Virgin, Our Price and Zavvi chains disappearing and even the once mighty HMV empire twice falling into administration. Thus, bizarrely, an exemption intended to help daffodil growers and farmers resulted in increased carbon emissions as CDs were ferried between the Channel Islands and the UK mainland, caused the

Government to lose tax income (an estimated £85 million [about US$110 million] per year in 2006) and contributed to the end of the high street record shop.[26] The Government eventually acted, ending this tax relief in April 2012, but it was too late for the hundreds of shops that had already closed.

If Benjamin Franklin is to be believed, other than taxes, death is the only thing of which we can be certain. However, he probably did not suspect that there could be a curious relationship between the two. In the late 1970s, the Australian Government abolished a tax on inheritances. As an extraordinary result, the death rate in the days approaching the changeover fell, with an appropriate increase in the death rate in the days following. It seems that about 1 in 20 of those dying were somehow able to delay their deaths just long enough to take advantage of the new rules.[27] Indeed, Australians appear to have extraordinary willpower for, at the other end of the spectrum, they were given only 7 weeks' notice that children born on or after 1st July 2004 would receive a "Baby Bonus" of A$3,000 (about £1,600 or US$2,100). Even with so little prior warning, mothers managed to delay the birth of their babies, with the result that 1st July 2004 was the birthdate of more Australian children than any day in the previous 30 years. It is estimated that over 1,000 births were "moved" (about a quarter by more than a week) so as to qualify for the payment. Admittedly, most of these were due to changes in the time of induction or Caesarean section procedures, but even so, it meant that a lot of mothers who had babies entirely naturally, when offered a cash incentive, were somehow able to postpone giving birth.[28]

The more complex a system is, the more it opens itself to unintended consequences, and the UK tax system certainly fits that bill. By 2009 the UK could boast that its tax code was the longest in the world, running to over 17,000 pages, or about 15 times the length of the Bible. There are around 1,100 different tax reliefs alone,[29] and a *Daily Telegraph* columnist was moved to observe that, "The tax system as it relates to corporate Britain has become wholly untenable. Its design and evolution is now one of such Byzantine complexity that nobody properly understands it. Like the hydra, close off one loophole and the system automatically generates others to take its place."[30] A perfect recipe for unintended consequences. But that sort of complexity is by no means necessary. In 1965/6 the equivalent volume was a mere 1/20 of the length at 759 pages, whilst the 2015 Hong Kong tax code, admired as the most efficient in the world, is just 276 pages.

Governments do have concerns other than economic ones of course. The freedom of their citizens is important to many, and in 2010 an Italian mayor was concerned that Muslim women were being forced by their husbands to wear the veil when they were out in public. He thus introduced a law to put a stop to this, banning any clothing that, "prevents the immediate identification of the wearer inside public buildings, schools and hospitals." In due course one woman, Amel Marmouri, was prosecuted for transgressing this law whilst standing in a post office queue. She was fined the equivalent of £430 (about US$560), but the result was that, rather than freeing her from the perceived restriction of the covering, her husband said that, "Now Amel will have to stay indoors. I can't have other men looking at her." So her freedom, and very likely that of other women in a similar position, has been further restricted as a consequence of a law that hoped to achieve the opposite.[31]

Equality is another much-vaunted goal of Western governments, but trying to impose it can be akin to grasping hold of a writhing eel. Requiring that companies take "affirmative action" to ensure that a minority group is not under-represented at senior level sounds all very well in theory, but as a 2014 American study has indicated, beneficiaries of this policy are often viewed as being less competent by their colleagues, which in turn creates self-doubt in their own minds. New York University's Professor Lisa Leslie observed that, "Diversity initiatives are effective, but also produce unintended consequences that can limit the career success of the very groups of employees they are intended to benefit." Her colleague Professor David Mayer, of the University of Michigan's Ross School of Business, went on to suggest that it was important to make very clear to everyone involved exactly how affirmative or positive action programmes worked. "A lot of people assume it's about hiring people less qualified because they are members of a protected group, even though that's illegal." As he pointed out, if people know that it's rather a case of widening the selection process, so that the job is made available to all, regardless of their race, sex or other defining characteristic, then it is "a totally different animal that few object to. Be transparent."[32]

Equality legislation may not only run the risk of having a detrimental effect on its recipients, but may even produce exactly the opposite of its intention. The 2010 UK Equality Act was supposed to create "equality of opportunity for all", and ensure that women should have the same opportunities as men. However, as BBC golf commentator Peter Alliss has observed, in the world of golf this has backfired, resulting in a reduction in the number of women taking part. As golf clubs were required (albeit sometimes grudgingly) to offer women the same membership terms as men, they have also been forced to stop the previously common practice of giving discounts to lady players. As a result, many women have found that they are now unable to afford the fees and have stopped playing. The Ladies Golf Union admitted that their membership had fallen from 189,000 in 2010 to 159,000 in 2014, although they claimed that there were other contributory factors as well.[33]

Most governments like to at least appear to have the best interests of their citizens at heart. But they can appear to be very secretive, and it was to counter this perception that in 2000 the Labour Government introduced the UK Freedom of Information Act. This gave ordinary citizens the right to obtain non-classified information from the authorities, but also meant that government departments might have to spend a great deal of time and effort in researching the answers to the requests for information, some of which they came to view as being merely vexatious.

One perhaps unusual duty carried out by the UK Government has been the recording of claims of UFO sightings, which since 1959 had been handled by a specific UFO monitoring unit based within the Ministry of Defence. However, after the unit was closed in 2010, a memo reported that any future reports would be "answered by a standard letter... retained for 30 days and then destroyed, largely removing any FoI liability." Quite understandably, the MoD does not wish to waste time and effort in answering what they see as pointless enquiries about reported UFO sightings. So, rather than retain correspondence which may in future be the subject of an information request, the Freedom of Information Act has encouraged them to destroy these reports, regardless of any value they might have. Whilst it is arguable that much of the information on this subject is of no value, it does not take a great leap to see that other departments may adopt the same approach, destroying potentially embarrassing material rather than running the risk of having it come into the public domain via the Act.[34] And sadly, if Britain is subsequently invaded by aliens, we may now never know about any of their earlier visits.

The Prime Minister's office took a similar approach to the MoD. Just before the Act was introduced, it instigated a default option whereby Downing Street emails were automatically deleted after 3 months unless they had been specifically saved. In addition, the possibility of the public reading their correspondence has made officials more nervous of committing their thoughts in writing at all, and meetings are held of which no written record is kept. As one special adviser commented, "It means that people don't remember things. It is dysfunctional. Then they check their emails and they don't exist anymore."[35]

Whilst "Freedom of Information" has brought real benefits and opened up the Government to scrutiny, it has also meant that in some areas there is less information to be made available, the public are no better informed and the Government itself is rather more confused about its decisions. Even political biographers, who may have thought that they would benefit from more access to information, may find that there is actually less of it in future. Charles Moore, the biographer of Margaret Thatcher, wrote that whilst researching his book, he had a welcome cornucopia of material, much of which was available online. However, he observed that with freedom of information laws in force, fewer people would be committing their truths to the written word. As writer Adam Gopnik has mused, "Instant transparency does not increase openness – it merely mutes conversation into corridors and off-the-record."[36] When we know that every written word may be subject to public scrutiny, we tend to be much more cautious about what we write.

Governments of major countries are, by their nature, unwieldy beasts, and can suffer from a lack of focus that can derail the worthiest of projects. In 1993, the British Government, noticing the imminent arrival of the Second Millennium, wished to do something special to mark this very special occasion. Their intention was to produce a grand project that would reflect the very best of Britain. The result, sadly, was something rather different.

A Millennium Commission of the great and the good was appointed to deal with the matter. However, over the next five years, the Commission saw a stream of Creative Directors and Government Ministers come and go. Finally, it was decided that the celebration would be in the form of a huge dome (the largest fabric structure in the world) on a piece of industrial wasteland in Greenwich, east London. It would be open throughout the year 2000 and would be filled with (at the time unspecified) wonders that would attract millions of people. The scheme would also regenerate this deprived area. But, as its architect Richard Rogers was later to say, "We had no idea what we were doing. No one did. The Tory government came up with the idea of a business pavilion, then Labour came in and decided it should be about entertainment and culture."[37]

Initially, the estimate for the number of visitors to the Millennium Dome (as it came to be known) was 12 million, but it quickly became apparent that this was an impossible dream. In fact, ticket sales over the course of the year amounted to only half that number and a mere £168 million (about US$218 million) of the £793 million (about US$1.03 billion) cost was recouped from ticket sales, sponsorship and merchandising, leaving the £625 million (about US$812 million) deficit to be picked up by the Government and National Lottery.[38] A survey indicated that 87% of the 6 million visitors were satisfied with their experience,[39] but the brutal fact remains that each of them had had their visit subsidised by over £100 (about US$130). To make things worse, the building itself then languished for a further four and half years, costing another £28.7 million (about US$37 million),[40] before it was rescued and transformed into the privately run O2 Arena, a concert venue which at last made a success of the structure.

As part of the plan to regenerate the area, about 1/3 of the Dome's cost had been spent on decontaminating its Greenwich Peninsula site, and investing in local transport links and infrastructure. However, ill-considered planning meant that some parts of the community were left worse off. In order to accommodate the world's first driverless bus, which was to ferry visitors from Charlton station to the Dome, a "transit interchange" was built. This resulted in the demolition of the only bank in Charlton, a major blow to the local community, but the scheme then fizzled out and the buses never ran.[41]

Intended to showcase the best of Britain, the Millennium Dome served perhaps only to indicate that Britain was a world leader in constructing ill-conceived white elephant projects. However, there were some successful enterprises associated with the Millennium. One of these was the "Millennium Wheel" (or London Eye as it came to be known), which conceptually was extremely simple – a glorified non-stop big wheel, 135 metres in diameter, placed on the banks of the River Thames and rotating once every 30 minutes. Conceived and planned by wife and husband team Julia Barfield and David Marks, it was originally to have only a 5-year lifespan, but such was its success that it has since become a permanent addition to the London skyline. The world's tallest Ferris wheel at the time of its opening (but usurped in 2014 by the High Roller in Las Vegas), it cost a comparatively paltry £70 million (about US$91 million) to build, and by the end of 2014 had carried 60 million passengers. As noted architect Sir Richard Rogers has written, "The Eye has done for London what the Eiffel Tower did for Paris, which is to give it a symbol and to let people climb above the city and look back down on it."[42] Its goal was simple, but it has achieved it splendidly.

Whilst the London Eye performed its one task very elegantly, another great Millennium venture had much wider ambitions. The Eden Project (which not only is *not* in London but is also quite a long way from anywhere else) was largely the result of businessman Tim Smit's visionary desire to follow his "Lost Gardens of Heligan" triumph with something on a grander scale. At Heligan the once splendid gardens had been completely neglected for 75 years until he, together with John Willis, a descendant of the original owners of the Estate, had transformed what had become a wilderness into a popular tourist attraction, bringing over 200,000 visitors each year to a relatively deprived part of the UK.

The Eden Project was a hugely ambitious plan to reproduce each of the Earth's ecosystems in an abandoned Cornish quarry, so that plants from every part of the world could be seen in something resembling their natural habitat. To do this, huge "biomes" (essentially golf ball-shaped greenhouses) were linked together, covering more than 5 acres of the site and rising to a height of almost 60 metres. Part-funded by the Millennium Commission, once it opened in March 2001, it was an immediate success, not only in terms of visitor numbers (it attracted over a million visitors a year, becoming the third most popular paid-for attraction in the whole country, despite its remoteness) but in raising awareness of the diversity of the world's plant life and the importance of plants to humankind. Having received £106 million (about US$138 million) in grants, mainly from Lottery funding, the EU and the Southwest Regional Development Agency, plus £20 million (about US$26 million) in commercial loans, in its first 10 years the project directly created 450 jobs in an area of high unemployment, as well as injecting an additional £1 billion (about US$1.3 billion) into the local economy.[43] Tim Smit has said that his vision for the Eden Project was, "To find the most derelict place on Earth and create life in it. We then wanted to show how clever human beings are, by building something totally fit for purpose, which I hope we did."[44]

If a lesson can be learned from contrasting these three Millennium projects, it would seem to be that, rather than appointing a committee to cold-bloodedly calculate what they think might be needed for a successful visitor attraction, it is much better to involve people who are passionate about a particular idea. George Bush, Sr. suffered throughout his presidency from what he described as a lack of "the vision thing"[45] and as Solomon noted many years ago in the book of Proverbs, "Where there is no vision, the people perish."[46] In the planning of the Dome, vision seems to have been very low on the agenda, whereas, as the *Economist* magazine put it, the Eden

Project "came out of a good idea looking for money, not money looking for an idea. Too many of the (Millennium) projects that got financed were born out of the determination of cities to get some of that lottery cash, no matter what it was for. Crucially, the Eden Project is essentially the vision of one entrepreneur."[47] The Eden Project's vision was to show people the wonders and interconnectivity of the world's plant life, or as Tim Smit put it, to "make science sexy".[48] The London Eye's vision, perhaps more prosaic, but compelling nonetheless, was simply to lift people up high enough to give them an aerial view of London.

An encouraging sign which suggests that organisations can perhaps learn from previous mistakes was the success of the opening and closing ceremonies for the 2012 London Olympics. On this occasion, rather than head up and control the events itself, the organising committee LOCOG swiftly handed the whole thing to a small team led by one man, film director Danny Boyle. The result was a completely maverick and inherently British event, bristling with confidence and yet full of humour and self-mockery. By their nature, governments tend to favour the po-faced, corporate and worthy, and it is well-nigh impossible to imagine any politician suggesting Eric Idle singing *Always Look on the Bright Side of Life* as a focal point for such a ceremony. The British Government was able to quietly bask in the reflected glory and the realisation that they had not messed this one up.

One of the problems that comes with being a government is that intractable problems seem to inevitably end up at your door. Following the launch of the then illegal download site Napster in 1999 and the subsequent rise of The Pirate Bay and other file-sharing websites, the entertainment industry saw huge amounts of potential revenue being lost due to the illegal copying of its music, films and games. It is almost impossible to gauge the true cost, but it is reckoned that the top 5 box office movies were illegally downloaded 1.4 million times in the UK in 2011 (a rise of 30% over 5 years), and that in 2010 there were an estimated 1.2 billion illegal song downloads in the UK alone (over 3 times the number of legal downloads).[49] In the same year it was estimated that four video games were illegally downloaded for each one legitimately purchased.[50] The industry in the UK has understandably applied pressure to the Government to "do something" about this, and so, in 2010 the UK Government introduced the Digital Economy Bill, which gave rights' owners new powers to act against illegal downloaders and the Internet Service Providers that hosted the infringing sites. A subsequent voluntary agreement has meant that these rights have by and large not been exercised, but it is worthwhile looking at what had happened in Sweden, where similar legislation had been introduced a year earlier. The government there had been pushed into action by the activities of The Pirate Bay, hugely popular around the world, but originally based in Sweden. The Swedish law came into effect in April 2009, following which overall Internet traffic in Sweden fell by a massive 30%, strongly suggesting that this practice was being curbed. However, within a few months, Internet activity had rebounded and then increased above the previous levels, and research by consultants MediaVision indicated that the accessing of illegally shared music, films and games had not only recovered, but that now a lot of it was encrypted, making it very much harder to track. The legislation had failed in its goal of reducing illegal activity and had led to the even bigger headache of untraceable file sharing.[51]

Western governments have steadily been attempting to outlaw different kinds of discrimination, but until 2011 it had been perfectly legitimate in the UK to dismiss workers simply because they had reached their 65th birthday. The Government then introduced legislation to outlaw discrimination on the basis of age, but certain employers, seeing this legislation approaching, took advance action. One of these was Longleat stately home, which had been happily employing 27 workers aged over 65, but which terminated their employment in the year before the legislation became effective, claiming though that the move was "unrelated to changes in the law", but had been done "to modernise the estate".[52] The one person unaffected was 78 at the time, but he was Lord Bath, the owner of Longleat. It does not seem unreasonable to suppose that without the legislation those workers would have continued to be employed for a number of years.

In a *New York Times* article, author Stephen Dubner and economist Steven Levitt highlighted a similar issue.[53] The Americans with Disabilities Act (ADA), introduced in 1992, prohibits discrimination against the disabled and attempts to improve their quality of life. However, research by economists Daron Acemoglu and Joshua Angrist discovered that once it came into effect there was actually a *drop* in the numbers of disabled workers being employed. Another economist, Sam Peltzman suggests that, before the ADA was introduced, employers would take a look at the possible costs and benefits of hiring a particular disabled person and, if they thought that, all things considered, they were the best person for the job, would employ them. However, after the ADA came into effect, it was down to the regulators to decide how the disabled person should be accommodated in the office and whether their wages were fair. If the employer then fires them because the costs of employing them are too high (or indeed, if they are just not up to the job), the employer lays themselves open to a claim for discrimination. The temptation is therefore for the employer to avoid that possibility by just not employing the disabled person in the first place.[54]

Another provision in the ADA entitled deaf people visiting the doctor to opt to have a signing interpreter on hand to help them. Dr Andrew Brooks, a top orthopaedic surgeon in Los Angeles, was asked to see a deaf patient who had a serious knee problem.

The patient said that she would like to have a sign-language interpreter present, but on discovering that the interpreter would cost US$120 (about £90) an hour, with a two-hour minimum, and would not be covered by insurance, Dr Brooks (who would only be paid US$58 [about £45] for the consultation) said that he would rather explain things himself through the use of drawings, models and notes. However, the patient then pointed out that, under the Act, she was entitled to choose the mode of interpretation at the doctor's expense, so the doctor was forced to engage and pay for the interpreter. Whilst the knee was physically painful for the patient, having to operate on it would become financially painful for the doctor. He would be paid approximately US$1,200 (about £920) but, with the likelihood of eight follow-up visits, and a US$240 (about £185) interpreter's fee each time, the doctor would be making a loss even before taking his clinical costs into consideration. Mercifully, Dr Brooks discovered that physical therapy was all that was needed to restore the knee (thereby transferring the costs issue to the therapist), but afterwards he discussed the case with medical colleagues. They all said to him that if they had a call from someone in that situation, they would never see them. It was clear that legislation which was intended to help disabled people to get the full medical help that they needed was in fact cutting them off from any help whatsoever. If doctors were forced to make a loss on a particular type of patient, then it is unsurprising that they would feel unenthusiastic about treating them.

From an outside perspective, it is easy to see that steps could have been taken to avoid this particular unintended consequence. The cost could have been covered by insurers, or the Government could have provided or paid for them. The cost would still have to have been met from somewhere, but at least the patient would get to see a doctor. As it was, everyone loses.

Even the tiniest of laws can result in unintended consequences.

For example, in 2011 a prison in Romania introduced a rule allowing 48-hour honeymoon visits for newlyweds. It has consequently seen an increase in the number of prisoners divorcing – in order to remarry their wives and qualify again as newlyweds. Some have divorced and remarried 4 times, but as Nicolae Toma, a spokesman for the prison admitted, "We cannot stop them, so they take advantage of the rules."[55]

Economic commentator Tim Harford has discussed the reasons why so often regulation fails to lead to the desired consequences.[56] He flagged up the example of falling standards in Parisian restaurants. In a move intended to improve matters, the French Government introduced a new symbol (a "saucepan-with-a-roof-and-chimney") to be used by restaurants to designate any dish that is made on the premises rather than being "bought in". So far, so simple. However, as Tim Harford pointed out, regulations are made by politicians, and politicians are subject to pressure by lobbyists. In this case, the industrial food companies took steps to protect their own interests and managed to ensure that the symbol could be applied even if the ingredients had been bought in, such as frozen fish and skinned and boned chicken, so long as the dish is actually "assembled" in the restaurant (even if that just means adding a home-made sauce). What diners wanted was good French food. However, what the regulation gave them was no more than a guarantee that the whole dish had not been made off-site, which is not necessarily the same thing at all. Worse still, because the symbol *must* be used where applicable, if only some of a restaurant's dishes are cooked on the premises, it may elect to drop those from its menu, because by using the symbol they draw attention to the fact that other items on their menu (which may actually be just as delicious) are not home-made in the same way. When writing the article, Tim Harford had just returned from holidaying in Italy, where he found the food was much better than in France. However, as he wryly mused, the credit for this should probably not go to the

Italian parliament.

Sometimes, governments don't even need to enact legislation in order to achieve an unintended result. In March 2012 UK fuel tanker drivers were threatening to strike, and the Government issued a reassuring statement suggesting that, whilst motorists should keep their tanks filled up, there was "no need to panic". As a perhaps inevitable result, drivers assumed that this meant that there was in fact *every* need to panic, and so queues formed at petrol stations all over the country. Garages struggled to cope with the resultant doubling or trebling in demand for fuel. Many ran dry, despite the fact that there was at that time as much fuel available as usual. Simon Wessely, a psychiatry professor at King's College London, said about this that, "The mistake is when someone says, 'Don't panic' ... Those who are already panicking don't hear it, and those who haven't panicked say, 'Well, hang on a second, there's obviously more to this than meets the eye. I was feeling all right until you told me, you're keeping something from me and things are worse than actually you're telling me.'"[57] Many will be reminded of a running joke in the BBC *Dad's Army* series, where Corporal Jones' automatic response in times of crisis was to run around yelling, "Don't panic!", thereby making things far more fraught. As Professor Wessely pointed out, drivers who make sure that they have a sufficient stock of petrol in times of shortage are not in fact panicking, but are acting in an entirely rational manner. He suggested that the course that governments ought to take is to give information without giving actual instructions – to have a policy of "Alert but not alarmed". It is when they tell the public not to panic that they generate the very behaviour that they are trying to avoid.

Irony is often the bedfellow of unintended consequences, and perhaps no more so than in the case of Plymouth University, which in 2014 put up posters in examination halls to remind students that they were not to cheat in their maths exam by, for example, writing formulae on their hands. The problem was that, in order to illustrate the issue, the University used a picture of a hand covered in mathematical formulae, some of which were, according to one student, useful for the exam. The University claimed that the posters were too far away to be of any practical use, but nevertheless removed them for the rest of the exam period.[58]

These examples amply illustrate the truth of economist Milton Friedman's 1975 statement that, "One of the great mistakes is to judge policies by their intentions rather than their results." So, if you have been invested with power and want to contribute to the general public good, some lessons seem to be:

Don't underestimate the ability of individuals to thwart your goals. If people can postpone birth or death for financial gain, give them a perverse incentive and there is almost nothing that is beyond them.

Try to look at the long-term repercussions of your decision. If, for example, you want to stop terrorists attacking your country, consider whether there might be better ways of achieving this than by conducting a "War on Terror".

If you are in a position of power, whatever you say is likely to be over-analysed and will almost inevitably cause people to overreact. So words should be chosen very carefully, and perhaps there might be occasions when the best course is to say or do nothing at all.

And finally, beware of appointing a committee to provide a solution – you run the risk of ending up with a Millennium Dome-scale disaster. Be open rather to the insight of inspired individuals.

Happily, there are times when even governments can manage

to resolve an unintended consequence. If we transport ourselves back to the year 1635, we can rejoice that the foundation of the Royal Mail has enabled us to send a letter throughout the United Kingdom. However, the cost of doing so was so high that all sorts of strategies were developed by those who wished to send post but avoid the expense. One of the more elegant was observed by the poet Samuel Taylor Coleridge whilst walking in the Lake District in 1822. He writes:

> *One day, when I had not a shilling which I could spare, I was passing by a cottage not far from Keswick, where a carter was demanding a shilling for a letter, which the woman of the house appeared unwilling to pay, and at last declined to take. I paid the postage; and when the man was out of sight, she told me that the letter was from her son, who took that means of letting her know that he was well: the letter was not to be paid for. It was then opened, and found to be blank!*[59]

The son, perhaps gone to the city or a country-house, wished to assure his mother that he was OK, but they both wished to avoid the extortionate cost of having a letter delivered, the shilling being demanded for delivery being the equivalent of almost £40 (about US$52) today! As the fee was paid on delivery, it became a common practice for those living a long way from home to send their loved ones an empty envelope every so often. After its cross-country journey, the postman would hand over the envelope, only for the recipient to note the identity of the sender and weigh it in their hand or hold it up to the light to see whether or not there was actually a letter inside. If not, they would hand it back and refuse delivery. The empty envelope itself was the message that all was ticking along smoothly at the other end, and only if there were some news would an actual letter be included. All very well for the correspondents, but the postal service had done all that work for nothing. It took the genius of Rowland Hill to turn the system on its head and convince the Government to introduce a prepaid postal system in 1840, which slashed the cost of sending a letter to a flat rate of a penny, regardless of distance.

* Indeed, the very name "War on Terror" brought unintended consequences, as Eliza Manningham-Buller (formerly head of MI5) has pointed out in her 2011 Reith Lectures. By claiming to be in a "War on Terror", the West made its oppressed opponents feel like "warriors", which was exactly what Al Qaeda wanted, and assisted them in gaining new recruits.

Chapter 2

"Why won't you do what we think is best for you?"

The abuse of dangerous drugs has long been an issue for society and governments. It would seem quite reasonable for governments to try to minimise harm to their populace, and they will often use legislation as a means of doing so. But drawing a line as to what is and what is not allowable under the law is often a contentious issue, and what is legal at one time in one place (including such commonplace drugs as alcohol, marijuana and LSD) may be illegal elsewhere, or even in the same country at different times.

One of the problems for governments is that they are never acting in a vacuum, but will be subject to the sometimes unreasonable and illogical views of their citizens. For example, tobacco has been exported from the US since the 1550s and is legally available worldwide, although subject to restrictions in many countries. However, it is estimated that 90% of all smokers are addicts, and it is claimed that addiction to nicotine can be just as powerful as to heroin and cocaine.[60] Tobacco is a very dangerous drug to use, with the World Health Organization reckoning that it causes over 5 million deaths worldwide every year and leads to more death and disability than any single disease. 90,000 of these annual deaths are in the UK, the equivalent of a good-sized plane crash at Heathrow every single day. If it were to be newly discovered today, tobacco's harmful effects and addictive nature would make governments very wary indeed of legitimising it. So, in an effort to improve matters, restrictions on its sale and use in the UK have been progressively tightened, and this, together with health campaigns and the introduction of electronic cigarettes, seems to be having some effect in reducing the harm caused by tobacco.

The other legalised recreational drug in everyday use in the West is of course alcohol. It is not as addictive as tobacco, but it is reckoned that 10% of regular drinkers are addicts. Directly or indirectly it results each year in an estimated 33,000 deaths in the UK and around 88,000 in the US.[61, 62] Liver disease, which is generally caused by alcohol abuse, killed 11,500 UK citizens in 2009 (more than 2½ times the figure for 1991), and is the only one of the "big killers" that is on the rise.[63] Worse still, alcohol is potentially lethal not only to the consumer, but also has repercussions for society as a whole, causing violence, family breakdown, lost productivity and general criminal behaviour. Quite apart from the emotional effect of being the victim of an alcohol-fuelled assault or robbery, it has been estimated that in 2011 these wider consequences were costing the UK economy each year about £3.5 billion (about US$4.5 billion) in NHS costs, £11 billion (about US$14.3 billion) in alcohol-related crime and £7.3 billion (about US$9.5 billion) in lost productivity, a total annual cost of almost £22 billion (over US$28 billion).[64] In the US, it has been estimated that in 2006 the total annual cost of excessive alcohol consumption was a massive US$223.5 billion (about £172 million).[65]

There is obviously a huge incentive for societies to reduce the harm caused by alcohol abuse. However, attempts to do so have been beset by unintended consequences.

Let us imagine ourselves in the US in 1913. At this time, American alcohol consumption was rising alarmingly, with annual production of beer surging from 1.2 billion to 2 billion gallons (about 4.5 to 7.5 billion litres) between 1900 and 1913, whilst sales of spirits rose from 97 million to 147 million gallons (about 367 to 556 million litres) per year in the same period. This was partly a result of a change in the ethnic make-up of the country, as immigration (especially from Europe) soared. In 1907 alone, over 1.2 million Europeans made America their new home. Many of the newcomers were from Germany and other countries with a heavy drinking culture, but even before their arrival alcohol had been a constituent part of American life for some time, with strong drink a requirement on every social occasion. The Old American Encyclopaedia described in 1830 that it was then the fashion to take a glass of whisky (flavoured with mint) upon waking, that office workers were let out both mid-morning and mid-afternoon for a glass of punch and that, come the evening, glasses of whisky or brandy were drunk prior to, during and after the meal.

Even clergymen threw themselves into the drinking culture. At every house call they would be offered drinks of rum and cider, and on leaving took a farewell drink for the sake of politeness. As they could make up to twenty such calls each day, there was every possibility that they would be completely inebriated by lunchtime. Churches and saloons were even built close together to enable the clergy and congregation to retire for a drink between services. All major church occasions were buoyed by alcohol, so that, for example, the mourners at the funeral of one preacher's widow in Boston managed to consume over 400 pints (about 230 litres) of fortified Malaga wine between them. Alcohol had become woven into every part of society, with community gatherings such as harvesting, road building or wood-cutting inevitably being followed by a binge. Workers even received part of their pay as liquor and were granted days off to get drunk.[66]

Rum, applejack and blackstrap (rum and molasses) cost only a few cents a quart (just over a litre), so that 19th century Americans, whatever their position in society, appear to have spent much of their lives in an alcoholic haze. Farm labourers (including slaves) were given ample liquor rations, whilst barrels of rum were available on tap in shops for favoured customers. The situation was very similar in the UK, the original home of many of the settlers, where pubs notoriously advertised that you could get, "drunk for a penny, dead drunk for twopence", and cheap gin wrought havoc amongst the poor.[67] As alcohol consumption rose, so did public disorder, illness and domestic violence.

By the time of the First World War, pressure from Temperance movements in the US had been steadily increasing, with the result that individual states had from time to time declared themselves "dry". With the end of the War, concern at the effect of alcohol abuse peaked, and beer became especially reviled, associated as it was with the hated Germans. This pressure eventually led to the passing of the Eighteenth Amendment to the US Constitution, prohibiting the manufacture, sale and transportation of intoxicating beverages, and so, in early 1920, Prohibition began.

Hopes were high for the new law. The well-known evangelist (and reformed alcoholic) Billy Sunday promised that, "The slums will soon be only a memory. We will turn our prisons into factories and our jails into storehouses and corncribs." Presuming that there would be a downturn in crime, some communities even went so far as to sell their jails.[68]

However, the reality was very different. The legislation did nothing to change human desires, and most drinkers wanted to carry on. The combination of a massive underlying demand for alcohol and a wide range of loopholes in the legislation encouraged a range of unintended consequences. With existing drink suppliers suddenly put out of business and unable to fulfil the demand, organised crime syndicates, already well established in the fields of prostitution and gambling, spotted an opportunity to move into a new market.

An obvious source of alcohol was America's neighbours. The US's border with Canada is the longest in the world (5,525 miles, or 8,891 km), and its southern border with Mexico runs for almost 2,000 miles (almost 3,000 km). Add the lengthy Atlantic and Pacific coastlines, and the difficulty of preventing contraband entering America is clear. With hardened drinkers prepared to pay premium prices for their favourite tipple, smuggling became a highly lucrative business. The Department of Commerce estimated that, by 1924, liquor valued at approximately US$40 million (a good US$400 million or £300 million in today's money) was entering the United States annually.[69] To replace the bars and saloons, speakeasies* sprang up all over the place as places where illicit liquor could be consumed. It has been suggested that for every saloon closed by Prohibition, half a dozen speakeasies appeared, and by 1925 there were believed to be as many as 100,000 in New York City alone[70] and up to half a million in the country as a whole.[71]

It also remained possible to obtain alcohol legitimately from within the US. Pharmacists were allowed to dispense whiskey for a huge number of ailments ranging from anxiety to flu. Bootleggers therefore moved into the pharmacy trade as a front for their business, with the result that the number of registered pharmacists in New York State tripled during the Prohibition era. Wine was also legally available through places of worship. As a consequence the number of self-professed rabbis rocketed, congregations at churches and synagogues rose and the amount of wine consumed for "sacramental purposes" increased by over 1/3 to almost 3 million gallons (over 11 million litres) in the two years to 1924. Whether this new-found religious fervour brought any spiritual benefit is uncertain.[72]

Sadly, rather than emptying the jails, Prohibition had just the opposite effect, with overall crime rising 24% during the Prohibition era. The number of prosecutions soared, and by 1930 almost eight times as many people were prosecuted for breaking the National Prohibition Act alone as had been charged with all federal crimes in 1914, and some half a million people were sent to prison during Prohibition for alcohol-related offences.[73] Murder rates had been rising since about 1906, but continued to rise during Prohibition, only to fall back quickly once Prohibition ended in 1933. Murder rates did not reach the same heights until the 1970s, a time when another prohibition – against drugs this time – was being much more actively enforced.[74] The Prohibition era was also the worst ever for police deaths, with an average of 250 officers being killed each year.[75]

The negative consequences of Prohibition continued way beyond its abolition. It glamorised lawbreaking and made it cool, bringing gangster culture into American mainstream. Gangster slang became part of everyday speech, so that one might be "bumped off" rather than murdered, pursued by "gumshoes" instead of detectives and not just carry a gun, but "pack a rod". Rum-runners became accepted as patriots, claiming that they were continuing the tradition of the smugglers who had broken the British blockades in colonial times. Captain Bill McCoy (who used the phrase "the real McCoy" to emphasise the purity of his wares) typified this type of character, evading the Coast Guard to run more than a million bottles of alcohol from the Caribbean to New York and acquiring a Robin Hood-like mystique in the process.

Prohibition also acted as a kind of "finishing school" for gangsters, enabling them, as historian Michael Woodiwiss has observed, to graduate from street gangs "to emerge as businessmen capable of running quite complex operations. Supplying middle- and upper-class demand for imported spirits, for example, required contracting for the liquor in sometimes distant countries, getting it past the Coast Guard and Customs, landing it on the docks, carting it to warehouses and delivering it to the retail outlets."[76] With the end of Prohibition, some bootleggers, such as Abner "Longy" Zwillman, turned to the legitimate distribution of liquor. With various partners he formed Browne Vintners to distribute alcohol in New York, selling the company 7 years later for US$7.5 million. However, many gangsters applied their new-found skills to enable them to expand other areas of their businesses such as drug smuggling, gambling and prostitution.

So criminality became worse rather than better under Prohibition, but how about people's health? Surely that would be improved by not drinking? Well, that was not quite how it turned out.

Many Americans, being practical folk, began producing their own alcohol, not only beer and wine but, much more lethally, spirits. Because it is so dangerous, there are strict health and safety laws governing the production of spirits, and teams of inspectors to ensure that all the proper procedures are being followed. Often cobbled together in hidden locations, illegal stills tend to operate on a much more casual basis. There is no official control over the ingredients used or the conditions in which the alcohol is produced, and with producers keen to minimise costs, corners will inevitably be cut in the production process. To make matters worse, as smaller quantities of liquid are easier to conceal, producers would often try to maximise the alcohol content in order to increase the value and minimise the risk before it was diluted for final sale. If drunk neat, this was extremely unhealthy, and very often even the dilutants themselves were harmful.[77]

Even worse, as the Government began to achieve some success in stemming the smuggling of alcohol, crime syndicates looked to other ways of obtaining it, and resorted to stealing legitimately produced industrial ethyl alcohol. This they obtained in huge amounts, with up to 60 million gallons (227 million litres) being stolen per year. Industrial alcohol is just ordinary grain alcohol, to which some unpleasant chemicals have been added to "denature" it and make it undrinkable, a practice that had originally been introduced in 1906 to prevent tax evasion. With the introduction of Prohibition, it suddenly became worthwhile for bootleggers to hire chemists to attempt to remove this contamination. The Government then tried to make it more difficult to clean, and added more and more disgusting ingredients, including kerosene, petrol, benzene, cadmium, mercury salts, formaldehyde, chloroform, carbolic acid, acetone and methanol. Drinking just three glasses of alcohol contaminated with methanol could lead to a horrible death. Removing all of these ingredients became all but impossible, but the criminals tended to go ahead and sell it anyway. As a result, on Christmas Eve in 1926 a man staggered into a New York hospital, deliriously claiming that Santa Claus was chasing him with a baseball bat. He died shortly after, followed by a further 30 people in New York over the following two days, all from drinking contaminated alcohol.[78] Indeed, it is estimated that by 1927 as many as 50,000 people had died throughout the country from drinking denatured alcohol, whilst hundreds of thousands were blinded or paralysed.[79]

Bizarrely, whilst Prohibition banned the purchase of alcohol, actually consuming it remained legal, so that wealthy people were able to buy up huge stocks of drink before Prohibition came in for consumption at a later date. Those with enough money bought up the stock of entire shops and even warehouses. The legislators themselves were no exception, so that in 1921, at the end of his term of office, President Woodrow Wilson transferred his stock of drink out of the White House to his new home, whilst the incoming President, Warren G. Harding, moved his in.[80]

The effect of Prohibition on existing distilleries, liquor brands and sellers of alcoholic drinks was inevitably devastating. Their businesses became almost worthless overnight, and the only people who were interested in buying them up tended to be of a criminal persuasion, who snapped them up very cheaply. Included in their assets was their existing stock of liquor, which could not be legally disposed of, but which their new criminal owners were able to sell on through various unorthodox or illegal channels, thereby netting themselves a huge profit.

The 1,300 breweries that had existed in 1916 had all closed within 10 years, and over the same period, the number of distilleries was cut by 85% (the remainder continuing to produce industrial alcohol). 314 wineries in 1914 had been slashed to 27 by 1925.[81] By banning the production and sale of alcohol and thus bringing about the destruction of legitimate businesses, the US Government had handed criminals a monopoly in a huge industry. These were people who were not bound by legal or moral constraints but were prepared to use any means and to go to any lengths in return for the massive profits that could be generated by meeting the continuing demand for alcohol.

As journalist Edward Behr has said, the effect of the era of Prohibition was to "transform the country's morals, alter American attitudes towards law enforcers, politicians and all those in authority, and herald a new mood of cynicism."[82] The cynicism was well-placed. Every layer of the justice system became corrupted, with members of the Government, the Prohibition Bureau and the police all receiving backhanders to assist the bootleggers, whether by issuing unofficial "permits" or just by looking the other way. They even provided official backup for liquor deliveries, deterring potential hijackers as well as reassuring customers as to the quality of the supplies and the unlikelihood of a police raid. It had become such a racket that at one time one of the major bootleggers, George Remus, was paying US$20 million in bribes per year to corrupt officials.[83] That was in 1920s money, so it would be worth a good US$200 million (over £150 million) today. As a measure of the extraordinary sums to be made from bootlegging, at the end of one of his parties, George presented each of the 50 female guests with a brand-new 1923 Pontiac car.[84]

As Paul Dickson has noted in his *Contraband Cocktails* book, "While deep in the Great Depression, the nation spent an estimated US$36 billion on bootleg alcohol, and the government had collected not a penny of this amount in excise taxes."[85]

So, crime and health both worsened as a result of Prohibition, but one might hope that Prohibition would at least have resulted in fewer people drinking. However, even on this count results were mixed, as although there was a slight decrease overall, people began drinking at an earlier age, and the total number of women who drank actually increased.[86]

Following the repeal of Prohibition, HL Mencken, whilst ladling on the hyperbole, wrote that:

> *Prohibition went into effect on 16 January 1920, and blew up at last on 5 December 1932 – an elapsed time of twelve years, ten months and nineteen days. It seemed almost a geologic epoch while it was going on, and the human suffering that it entailed must have been a fair match for that of the Black Death or the Thirty Years War.*[87]

Prohibition even had a knock-on effect on the restaurant business. Being reliant for much of their profits on the sale of wine, many fine restaurants were unable to continue as a going concern and thus folded, whilst others felt that to eat excellent food without the accompaniment of wine was so unthinkable that they closed on this point of principle.[88] They were replaced by the speakeasies, where food was a very low priority, and thus another industry, and those who relied on it for a living, was brought down by Prohibition and handed (almost literally) on a plate to the criminal fraternity.[89]

There were arguably, however, a couple of upsides to Prohibition. One was the establishment of the cocktail drink. Popularised during Prohibition as a means of disguising the disgusting taste of home-made gin or flavoured wood alcohol, it has evolved and flourished ever since.[90] The cocktail shaker became a necessity, largely because "that synthetic stuff has to be chilled to the limit and whipped to a lather, in order to get rid of the liniment taste and make it resemble something to drink" as George Ade suggests in his 1931 classic *The Old-Time Saloon*.[91]

Stock car racing too can trace its roots back to Prohibition. Moonshine runners needed to have nippy cars to escape from the police whilst making their deliveries. Unsatisfied with the vehicles of the day, they went to the lengths of building special small cars which could go very fast and could outmanoeuvre and outrun the police. As the numbers of these cars increased, so did competition between the various manufacturers and drivers, and they began to organise informal races. Initially very secretive affairs, spectators soon thronged to see these events, leading to the sport being formalised in 1948 with the formation of NASCAR, since when stock car racing has become one of the totemic American sports.

Whilst the outright banning of alcohol has led to many unintended consequences, even just imposing taxes on it may not be unproblematic. If prices rise too high, there remains the temptation to produce one's own poteen and other home-made spirits. This still goes on in the UK, and the dangers of doing so became apparent in July 2011, when a group of men were operating an illegal vodka distillery in a warehouse on an industrial estate in Boston, Lincolnshire. With secrecy paramount, the lack of ventilation allowed highly inflammable alcohol vapour to build up in the confined space, so that, when one worker lit a cigarette, the whole building exploded with a massive blast that was heard up to five miles away. The warehouse was completely destroyed, and five of the six workers were killed.[92, 93] And in the week following that explosion, a raid on an industrial unit in the centre of Birmingham discovered another illegal vodka distillery. Amongst the material seized were over 2,500 litres (over 660 gallons) of so-called "Arctic Ice" vodka and thirteen 1,000 litre (264 gallon) bulk containers, three of which contained 96% industrial alcohol. As was so often the case during Prohibition, the vodka itself was unfit to drink as it contained dangerous levels of methanol, and again, the lack of safety measures meant that there was a high risk of an explosion. Three men were later convicted of evading nearly £500,000 (about US$650,000) in excise duties.[94]

Governments are constantly trying new methods of reducing alcohol abuse. As well as imposing taxes and duties to increase its price, they may apply more nuanced financial strategies, such as restricting "Happy Hour" offers or imposing a minimum price per unit of alcohol. Physical barriers may also be imposed, such as in parts of Canada, where alcohol may not be sold in a supermarket, but only via a shop with a separate entrance, presumably hoping that this will dissuade impulse purchases and make regulation easier.

Continental Europe has long been felt to have had a fairly comfortable relationship with alcohol, the United Kingdom less so, and Scotland a particularly uneasy one. In 2009 the Scots outdrank the English and Welsh per head by almost a quarter, but it is not merely the quantity of alcohol consumed that is an issue, but the circumstances in which it occurs. Thus, on a typical Saturday night in Glasgow, over a thousand people will be admitted to accident and emergency units, mainly as a result of drinking too much themselves or having been assaulted by others who have. Rates of alcohol-related deaths in Scotland are about twice those south of the border, whilst drink is a factor in about half of all homicides. However, as the post-2008 recession began to bite, alcohol became less affordable for young people, contributing to a 30% fall in serious violent crime between 2009 and 2014. Jonathan Shepherd, the director of Cardiff University's violence and society research group, which carried out the investigation, warned, however, that violence on the streets could increase again if an economic recovery meant that alcohol became more affordable and he therefore recommended keeping it comparatively pricey by imposing minimum unit pricing.[95]

However, rather than attempting to stop people drinking, Glasgow has introduced a scheme that approaches the problem from a different angle. Teams of so-called "street pastors" walk the streets at night, having been trained in first aid, sociology and criminology, with the aim of alleviating the problems that can arise from intoxication. Originating with a trial in deprived areas of London, Birmingham and Manchester, street pastors (all of whom are drawn from local churches) act as a calming influence, engaging with people out on the streets at night and helping to defuse potentially difficult situations. Their role is not to enforce the law or stop people drinking, but rather to offer help and advice if needed. They also offer practical help such as handing out bottles of water and giving flip-flops to girls who have become unable to walk in their high heels. Their attitude is that just having someone available for a bit of friendly conversation is important and helpful.[96] This approach seems to be meeting with some success in reducing the after-effects of intoxication. Detective Chief Inspector Teresa Russell of the City of London Police has said that, "Experience has shown that the presence of these schemes...has had a positive effect in bringing a measure of calm to otherwise rowdy situations",[97] and one area of Kingston-upon-Thames, in the south-west of London, has seen violent offences fall by half in the first five years of the scheme's operation.[98] Since beginning in 2003 street pastor schemes have been set up in some 250 places around the UK and it has been praised by police and politicians alike, with the then Prime Minister David Cameron enthusing in 2008 that, "It's absolutely fabulous the job the street pastors are doing."[99]

As well as alcohol, there are of course many other drugs that have an effect on the human body, whether it be stimulating, narcotic and/or hallucinogenic. Some, such as caffeine, are entirely legal in the UK, whilst nicotine is readily available over-the-counter, albeit with certain restrictions. Others, including cannabis, ecstasy, heroin, cocaine and many more are prohibited altogether. However, as we saw with alcohol, banning something does not necessarily reduce demand, and can open the door to a range of unintended negative consequences. The United Nations Office of Drugs and Crime has recognised this, and has highlighted five problem areas.

The first is that, as with Prohibition, a huge criminal black market is created. The cost of producing a kilo (2.2 pounds) of cocaine is an estimated US$2,000 (about £1,500) from leaf to lab, whilst the street value of that kilo in the US is anywhere between US$34,000 (about £26,000) and US$120,000 (about £92,000), depending on where it is sold, so the financial incentives are self-evident. Most of these profits end up in the hands of organised crime gangs and terrorist organisations, for whom the trafficking of illegal drugs has become a core fund-raising activity.

The second is referred by the UN as "policy displacement". Although public health and prevention campaigns have a vital role to play in solving the drug problem, huge efforts are put into the enforcement of drug laws, absorbing a huge amount of finite government resources which could otherwise have gone into health or other programmes. This is something that the viewers of the acclaimed TV series *The Wire* have seen graphically illustrated. The programme is set in the American city of Baltimore, where the police have so concentrated their efforts on the drugs trade that there has been a huge fall in the prosecution of other crimes, even major offences such as murder, rape and aggravated assault.

The third unintended consequence may be called the balloon effect. Thus, when pressure was applied to squeeze the supply of Chinese opium in the middle of the 20th century, production simply shifted, boosting production in the "Golden Triangle", comprising Vietnam, Laos, Thailand and parts of Burma. Then, when there was crackdown in Thailand, Burmese production grew further, and efforts to prevent opium growing in Turkey, Iran and Pakistan eventually displaced the problem to Afghanistan, where the crop continues to act as a fund-raiser for the Taliban, with "taxes" levied on the trade bringing them in at least US$400 million (over £300 million) per year.[100] Fourthly, there is what the UN refer to as "substance displacement", meaning that when the authorities concentrate on action against one drug, suppliers and users will move on to another drug with similar effects but looser controls. Thus, if a blitz is conducted against cocaine, users may switch to amphetamines, which are harder to control as they can be produced locally (even in a kitchen), rather than having to be imported from South America.

The final issue that they addressed was the stigmatising of drug users, which tends to isolate them and restrict their society to that of other drug users, so that even those who want to give up drugs may find themselves sucked back in by their drug-using friends.[101] And although friends may attempt to help, that may not be enough. Thus, although the family of billionairess and drug-addict Eva Rausing spent £100,000 (about US$130,000) each month employing an eight-man team of former SAS members to watch over her and scare away her drug dealer contacts, she still managed to gain access to cocaine and other drugs, resulting in her death in May 2012 in squalid surroundings in her £5 million (about US$6.5 million) London house.[102]

As it did with the original Prohibition, the United States provides a fine example of how these various unintended consequences can work themselves out. In the 1980s and 90s, most drugs coming into the US originated in Colombia and its South American neighbours. They were transported by a variety of routes, either directly by boat, plane or even submarine, or overland via Mexico. In response, the US Government committed an annual budget of US$12 billion (£9 billion) to the problem, launching a huge military operation to stop the smugglers, using fighter jets to take control of the skies and Navy submarines to patrol the seas. Pressure was applied to the Colombian Government in an attempt to disrupt the manufacturing process, as well as to apprehend gang leaders such as the notorious Carlos Escobar. With the death of Escobar in 1993 and the subsequent capture or killing of the 15 other drug kingpins on their "Most Wanted" list, the Americans felt that a real advance had been made in their war on drugs. However, with the removal of their leaders, the gangs fractured into "micro-cartels" and changed their means of delivery to the US. They concentrated their efforts into smuggling overland through Mexico. They were unintentionally assisted in this by the 1994 North American Free Trade Agreement, which freed up trade with Mexico and led to a huge increase in goods of all sorts flooding over the Mexican/US border, making it much harder to check exactly what was coming in. As Steve Robertson, a member of the Drug Enforcement Agency assigned to southern Texas, observed at the time, on just one road there were, "A thousand trucks coming across in a four-hour period. There's no way we're going to catch everything."[103] And so a variation on the "balloon effect" meant that, as one direct pipeline was cut off, the supply merely shifted via the next available route.

As the drugs trade concentrated on Mexico, the way of doing business changed. The Mexicans involved decided that they weren't prepared to accept just the role of smugglers and gradually began to take control of the whole production line. The operation became much more professional, so that, for example, the cocaine trafficker Amado Carrillo Fuentes employed lawyers and accountants and developed a transportation division (which included a fleet of Boeing 727s to fly cocaine from Colombia to Mexico), as well as an acquisitions division and even a human resources department. His organisation was set up like a legitimate corporation and was reminiscent of the way in which alcohol bootlegging operations were run 70 years earlier in the Prohibition Era.[104]

As the business expanded, earnings grew, to such an extent that in 2009, an American Justice Department report estimated that the drugs trade was generating an annual profit of up to US$39 billion (about £30 billion). With this amount of money at stake, the gangs became more ruthless as they sought dominance in the market. The Mexican Government responded to the violence by bringing in the military, and by 2010 Mexican President Felipe Calderón had mobilised 45,000 troops in addition to the regular police force.

In areas where the gangs were active, the situation became desperate. The turf wars between the cartels resulted in more than 100,000 drug-related murders between 2006 and 2013. Although gang members accounted for about 90% of these deaths, police, soldiers, elected officials (including 14 mayors), journalists and uninvolved bystanders were also victims.[105] As the warfare became ever more brutal, the gangs took advantage of the low levels of army pay by offering soldiers of all ranks huge pay rises and employing them to help the gangs with their security. Perhaps the deadliest and most brutal of the drug gangs has been Los Zetas, whose leaders were originally special forces operatives and army officers fighting *against* the drug barons, but who, having been offered massive salary increases, became guns for hire and enforcers for the Gulf drug cartel. Then, seeing where the real money was, they formed their own gang. Whilst Gulf relied on bribery to achieve its goals, Los Zetas has become known for its extraordinary brutality. "Because of its quasi-military background, cold-blooded killing is what they know best," says Victor Guerrero, a former Mexican federal policeman. "It was Los Zetas who introduced the method of abduction, torture, beheading and dismemberment of its enemies as a means of intimidation." They even recruited gang members by force, sometimes abducting illegal immigrants from buses and executing any who refused to work for them.[106]

In attempting to counter the drugs trade by military means, the Mexican Government has inadvertently contributed to the establishment of a group that ratcheted up the violence to a completely new level. And despite the US Government spending more than a trillion dollars on the war on drugs since 1971, the US remains the world's largest buyer of illegal drugs.[107] Things have not gone according to plan.

Frighteningly, this ratcheting up of violence seems now to have spread to Britain. Neil Woods was an undercover British policeman who infiltrated drugs gangs and had them sent to jail. However, as he and his colleagues became steadily more successful, he found that the violence being meted out by the gangs against suspected informers was being steadily escalated. In Northampton, the girlfriend or sister of an informant would be gang-raped, whilst in Brighton, dealers would spike the heroin so that it would kill the user. For him, this explained why the fatality rate amongst heroin users in Brighton was five times the national average. As he said, "The most efficient way to stop people grassing is to become terrifying. In other words, organised crime groups were getting nastier and nastier as a direct result of what I was doing." He went on, "Brighton is the thin end of the same wedge destroying Mexico. Mexico's just the thicker end of it, but it can only go in one direction."[108]

The approach that the Americans and Mexicans have taken to solve the drug problem is to attempt to reduce the supply, but, as any economist will happily point out, unless the demand is reduced as well, any success in reducing the supply will merely force up prices, fuelling an increase in crime as addicts take more and more desperate measures to find the money to buy their supplies.

Even in countries which avoid the horrors of Mexico, there will naturally be a close relationship between drugs and crime, whether through addicts needing to steal to fund their habit or just because the trade has been criminalised. In the UK, it has been estimated that as much as a fifth of all crime could be related to drugs, at a huge cost in policing and imprisonment, to say nothing of the misery of the victims.[109] America has certainly cracked down on those involved in the drugs trade and, just as with Prohibition, there has been a huge increase in the number of people in prison. By 2008, fully 1% of the US adult population was in prison (and over 6% of black adult men),[110] and between

2001 and 2013, one half of prisoners serving sentences of more than a year in federal facilities in the US had been convicted of drug offences.[111]

Cracking down hard on drug-takers and sending them to prison can itself have counterproductive effects. If not given appropriate support and treatment, they will be released from prison with the same (and quite possibly worse) problems, reducing their chances of recovery.[112] And not only does imprisoning drug users cost the government huge amounts of money in keeping people in prison, but it results in otherwise law-abiding young adults receiving a criminal record, thereby limiting their career prospects and possibly resulting in a downward spiral of unemployment and involvement in petty crime. Any civilised government wants to help its citizens to achieve their best, both for the benefit of themselves and society as a whole, and criminalising a large group of young people is not helpful in achieving that goal.

And taking drug dealers off the street is not a guarantee that conditions will improve. As the 2012 UK Drug Policy Commission Report observed, arresting one group of drug dealers may well lead to an increase in violence as rivals attempt to exert their influence. Thus, in Enfield in North London, the police undertook a major operation which resulted in dozens of gang members being jailed. But the result was actually an increase of violence on the streets and an upsurge in knife attacks, as gangsters from surrounding areas sought to take advantage of the power-vacuum, whilst younger recruits wanted to prove their ruthlessness.[113] However, adopting a more nuanced approach, targeting drug dealers who were particularly violent or exploited children, whilst giving smaller-scale drug dealers the option of support to help them change their lives, has proved successful in reducing the harm to some communities.[114]

One issue which the UN report did not draw particular attention to, but which we saw as a problem in the Prohibition era, was that the illicit production of substances is not conducive to the health of the consumers. This applies just as much to illegal drugs, which are not tested for purity by any reputable agency, and even the most scrupulous of drug dealers will not know how the drugs have been treated on their often long and circuitous journey. Combining drugs with other, less expensive materials is an easy way to increase profit margins, and thus additives such as lead, strychnine, aluminium and glass, as well as various chemicals, have all been used as adulterants,[115] bringing their own particular dangers when ingested by the human body.

As well as deliberate pollution, there is also the danger of accidental contamination of drugs en route to the end user. In 2009, health officials in Glasgow were mystified by an outbreak of anthrax, a disease that had almost been eradicated throughout the world. Upon investigation, it became apparent that all of the victims were drug addicts who had injected heroin which had somehow become contaminated with anthrax. The authorities concluded that the anthrax had probably been acquired when a batch of heroin was smuggled through Turkey hidden in the skin of a goat that had carried the anthrax spores in its stomach. During the outbreak, 13 people died in Scotland, as well as 4 in England and 1 in Germany.[116]

As President Obama admitted at a Summit of the Americas in 2012, "it is entirely legitimate to have a conversation about whether the laws in place are doing more harm than good in certain places,"[117] and the situation was perhaps best summarised in 2013 by Stephen Rolles, Senior Policy Analyst with the Transform Drug Policy Foundation, who stated that, "The war on drugs, like US alcohol prohibition, has been an unmitigated disaster. It has, however, achieved a great deal for the gangsters that now control a market worth £260 billion (about US$338 million) a year, not to mention corrupt officials, prison builders and money-laundering banks who've all profited hugely from this 50-year folly."[118]

Having recognised the varied unintended consequences of trying to curb drug abuse through legal constraints, almost 100 countries are now trying to help those affected by trying out "harm reduction". This policy emerged in the 1980s as governments tried to quell the epidemic of HIV amongst injecting drug users. To cut down the spread of disease by the use of shared needles, single-use syringes have been provided free of charge to addicts, and facilities provided for the disposal of used needles. This practice has spread outside obviously deprived areas, and in 2012 a needle disposal bin was installed in the comparatively well-to-do market town in Sussex where I live, in the professed hope that this would do more good than harm. This approach had helped to ensure that by 2012, the HIV rate amongst injecting drug users in the UK was one of the lowest in the world.[119]

The policy of harm reduction has led a number of countries to decriminalise the possession of small amounts of drugs for personal use. The Netherlands, Portugal, Argentina, Uruguay, the Czech Republic and Mexico have all changed the emphasis from the criminalisation of drug users towards therapy to help them off drugs.

And the potential benefits of some form of legalisation are huge. When Uruguay legalised cannabis in 2013, it did so in the expectation that this would lead to up to £25 million (about US$33 million) per year being diverted from criminal networks[120] (although four years later its effectiveness in this respect was still unclear), whilst in 2016, the Liberal Democrat party claimed that legalising cannabis could raise £1 billion (about US$1.3 billion) annually in tax for the UK Government.[121]

One US state has already begun to reap the financial benefits. It is one of four American states that, by 2016, had licensed the production and sale of cannabis. The four were Colorado, Alaska, Oregon and Washington (as well as the District of Columbia, despite the objections of the White House), whilst almost half of all US states had legalised it for medical purposes.** Colorado's legislation came into effect at the beginning of 2014, and by early 2016 cannabis had become a US$1 billion (about £770 million) per year industry. In 2015 the state received US$135 million (about £104 million) in cannabis taxes and fees – about 3 times the taxes collected on alcohol. There is a very strict licensing regime in place, requiring that every individual plant grown is electronically chipped so that the state can track it, and by testing the cannabis for potency and contaminants, the state ensures that quality is maintained and purchasers know exactly what they are buying.[122, 123] Asked about the effect of the legalisation of cannabis, a Denver police officer summed it up as, "The sky isn't falling." He went on to say that crime rates had been dropping in Denver prior to legalisation, and that the trend had continued.[124]

We should not, however, be lulled into thinking that all is sunshine and lollipops in Colorado. Although legalised at state level, under Federal law cannabis remains a restricted drug. This confusing legal status has made the Colorado police uncertain about exactly which laws they should enforce, whilst banks are extremely fearful of dealing with cannabis producers, making it very difficult for drugs-related businesses to even open an account, and next to impossible to borrow money to finance growth.[125]

Whilst it might be expected that this slackening of legal constraints would lead to an increase in drug usage, in Portugal, following decriminalisation in 2001, use amongst school-age children has actually fallen, whilst cannabis use is no more prevalent in the Netherlands, where its use is licensed, or in US states that have decriminalised it, than in their neighbouring countries or states, although in Colorado the rate of drug use among the young, though falling, is still the highest of any US state.[126] As a World Health Organization report points out, "Globally, drug use... is not simply related to drug policy, since countries with stringent user-level illegal drug policies did not have lower levels of use than countries with liberal ones."[127]

Decriminalising the production of cannabis has, as one would hope, vastly reduced the demand for the drug from illicit sources, consequently reducing the income and power of criminal gangs. According to a *Time* magazine report, seizures of cannabis being imported into the US from Mexico fell from 1,250 tons in 2011 to 950 tons in 2014, whilst the fall in Mexico itself has been even steeper, with 664 tons seized in 2014, a fall of 32% from a year earlier. Violent deaths in Mexico have also fallen, from a high in 2011 of almost 23,000 to 15,649 in 2014.[128]

The Colorado policy of licensed production and sale of cannabis on a free-market basis is but one possible way of approaching this issue, and a 2014 report by the London School of Economics' Expert Group on the Economics of Drug Policy, a group which included five winners of the Nobel Prize in Economics, suggested that:

> The debate over how to legalise cannabis tends to assume that for-profit commercial enterprise is the default option. Legalising cannabis on the alcohol model may, however, be the second-worst option (behind only continued prohibition); commercialisation creates an industry with a strong incentive to promote heavy use and appeal to minors through aggressive marketing. No system of legal availability is likely to entirely prevent an increase in problem use. But pioneering jurisdictions should consider alternative approaches including non-profit regimes and state monopoly. Both sides of the legalisation debate should acknowledge that the question is complex and the range of uncertainties wide. Such modesty, alas, is in short supply.[129]

Ending the war on drugs could bring other benefits to developing countries. Whilst farmers may be offered development aid to stop growing opium poppies, coca, cannabis or similar crops, in order to access that aid they will be obliged to destroy their plants in advance, thus depriving them of their entire year's income before the promised aid is paid through. As if that weren't sufficient disincentive, often the sprays used to destroy the crops damage the local environment. As Wilder Mora Costa, a Colombian farmer, put it, "The environment suffers, water is contaminated and fish die."[130] However, many of these plants that the farmers grow have medicinal uses, and if foreign governments were to consider buying the drugs from the farmers rather than trying to destroy them, they could put them to use for legitimate means. This would remove the farcical situation where governments are paying to destroy crops grown in one part of the world whilst encouraging different farmers to grow them in another. For example, whilst the UK supports the spraying with weed killer of opium poppies in Afghanistan, they are currently being cultivated on an estimated 6,300 acres of UK farmland. It would seem to make much more sense to buy the crop from Afghan farmers, supporting their local community by trade rather than aid, and at the same time removing their crops from the illegal supply chain. The farmland that is currently being used to grow poppies in the UK could easily be turned to other uses, so surely everybody wins.[131]

The 2014 LSE report damningly summed up the effect of the War on Drugs thus:

> The pursuit of a militarised and enforcement-led global "war on drugs" strategy has produced enormous negative outcomes and collateral damage. These include mass incarceration in the US, highly repressive policies in Asia, vast corruption and political destabilisation in Afghanistan and West Africa, immense violence in Latin America, an HIV epidemic in Russia, an acute global shortage of pain medication and the propagation of systematic human rights abuses around the world.[132]

Having seen the terrible results of Prohibition on American

society, very few democratic governments have felt that problems with alcohol are best solved by banning it. However, it is interesting that relatively few appear to see a parallel between alcohol and drug abuse, and would still prefer to ban any drugs which are seen to be dangerous.

Frustratingly, whilst legalising drugs can reduce some unintended consequences, some others can result from the policy. As we have seen, with the relaxation of cannabis legislation in some US states and the consequent increase in availability of high quality US-grown cannabis, the demand for supplies smuggled from Mexico has fallen. All well and good, but in line with the UN's "substance displacement" theory, Mexican drug cartels have turned their attention to harder and more dangerous drugs such as heroin and methamphetamine, with the result that, between 2008 and 2015, seizures of meth tripled in Californian ports of entry, and across the south-west border, seizures of crystal-meth hit a new high in 2014,[133] whilst heroin seizures doubled in the five years to 2015.[134]

As the 2014 LSE Report concluded:

The United Nations has for too long tried to enforce a repressive, "one-size-fits-all" approach. It must now take the lead in advocating a new cooperative international framework based on the fundamental acceptance that different policies will work for different countries and regions.

This new global drug strategy should be based on principles of public health, harm reduction, illicit market impact reduction, expanded access to essential medicines, minimisation of problematic consumption, rigorously monitored regulatory experimentation and an unwavering commitment to principles of human rights.[135]

Neil Woods, the former undercover policeman quoted earlier, felt so strongly about the adverse effects of his own job that in 2015 he became the UK chair of Law Enforcement Against Prohibition, an international organisation comprising people involved in the police, military, prison service and intelligence agencies who want to pass on to the public their first-hand knowledge of how damaging the war on drugs has been. Remarkably, Woods was diagnosed with a particular form of PTSD called Moral Damage, brought on by the realisation that not only was he failing to improve matters, but that his work was actually contributing to the misery that he saw. His conclusion is that rather than resort to legislation, drugs such as heroin should be prescribed by doctors to addicts under strictly regulated conditions, so that, "drug policy should be about reducing not drug use, but drug harm."[136]

* So called because patrons were encouraged to "speak easy" when at the bar, so as not to give any indication that alcohol was being consumed.

** Although the definition of "medical" can be somewhat elastic, as journalist Hugo Rifkind, walking on Venice Beach in Los Angeles, discovered in 2012. A man wearing green surgical scrubs rolled past him on a skateboard, enquired as to his ailment and had just the one remedy to offer – marijuana, at US$50 a prescription.[358]

Chapter 3

How can I stop screwing up?

Sometimes, we are so conscious of the need to do the right thing, that we end up doing exactly the opposite. When much younger, a group of us attended a party at the very posh house of a friend of a friend. All I remember of the party is that the whole house had cream carpets and that the drink du jour was red wine. Although (in fact I suspect that *because*) we were all too aware of the dire consequences of one coming into contact with the other, the inevitable occurred, and most of the evening was spent attempting to restore the carpet to something like its original state.[137] Renowned Harvard psychologist Daniel Wegner referred to this kind of mistake as a "precisely counter-intuitive error", as we screw up precisely because we are trying so hard *not* to.

A similar problem can occur in our love-lives. The four protagonists in the TV series *Sex and the City* could surely have settled into happy relationships quite easily, had it not been for their continual habit of over-thinking and over-analysing every potential mate, rather than just going with the flow and seeing how things turned out.

Parents will be only too aware of the perils of interfering in a relationship of which they disapprove. The story of Romeo and Juliet reflects a painful truth. By placing so many barriers in the way of the young couple in an attempt to end their relationship, their families may well have turned a merely juvenile infatuation into an all-consuming passionate affair, resulting in tragedy rather than a relationship which fizzled out of its own accord. A study of 140 couples in Colorado indicated that parental interference does indeed have this effect. As external pressure to end a relationship increased, so did the couple's strength of feelings for each other.[138]

Whilst too much pressure on people in a relationship can bring them closer together, for lonely people, the opposite may be true. It is easy to assume that the friendless are in that state because of a lack of social skills. In fact, research has discovered that the social skills of the lonely may actually be better than those who seem more gregarious. In a test that they were told was purely theoretical, lonely people were better at accurately interpreting facial expressions and tone of voice. However, when they were put under pressure by being told that people who did poorly in this task tended to have problems establishing and maintaining relationships, they did worse than the naturally gregarious. It appears to be that it is often not so much a question of ability, but of performance anxiety. The lonely may be so keen to form relationships that they hyper-focus on not screwing-up, resulting in over-thinking and second-guessing, which sadly leads to the screwing-up that they are so intent on avoiding. One possible solution is to try to re-imagine nervousness as excitement, turning dread into anticipation. This may be difficult to achieve, but it is surely helpful for the lonely to realise that they do have the ability to deal with tricky social situations, and that they just need to put them into practice.[139]

Daniel Wegner called this type of pressure "mental load", when our minds become so stressed with the effort of suppressing a thought or action that we react in exactly the manner we dreaded.[140] This can be comedic (if painful) for onlookers. The "Gourmet Night" episode of the UK sitcom *Fawlty Towers* has hotelkeeper Basil Fawlty giving a perfect example. He is extremely satisfied to have attracted the cream of Torquay society to his Gourmet Evening. The pressure of knowing that he must be on his best behaviour means that things misfire from the very beginning. One of his guests, a Mrs Hall, is tiny, and the obsequious Basil becomes consumed with the idea that to make reference to this would be a terrible faux pas. Having inadvertently addressed her as Mrs *Small* on one occasion, he knows that to repeat this error would be unforgivable. So, when asking her what size drink she would like, he is forced to tap-dance frantically, asking her if she would like a, "Large, or... or... or not quite so large?" The evening spirals disastrously downhill from there.

Sport is particularly prone to this problem, with the "yips" being a well-known phenomenon to golfers. When preparing to putt or drive, it is easy to concentrate so much on achieving a smooth action that an arm inadvertently jerks at the vital moment, sending the ball skittering away. The term was coined by Tommy Armour, who in 1927 won the US Open. Just one month later, playing the Shawnee Open, he managed to achieve the highest single-hole score by a professional, a truly impressive 23 shots, for which he blamed "the yips".

Perhaps golf's most infamous case of the yips though is Greg Norman's ill-fated final round at the 1996 US Masters. With 18 holes to play, the world number one was 6 shots ahead of Britain's Nick Faldo. He had played beautifully over the first 3 days, but from the beginning of the final round he looked out of sorts, and dropped 2 shots to Faldo over the first 8 holes. Then, as *Sports Illustrated* recounted at the time, Greg Norman played the most catastrophic four holes in his life. On the 9th, he chipped hopelessly short of the pin and dropped a shot. On the 10th he missed a simple uphill chip and then missed the 8-foot putt. At the 11th, he missed his putt from 3 feet, and the players were level. Then at the 12th, he hit a double-bogey, his fifth straight 5.

By the time the final putt was sunk, his 6 shot lead had become a 5 shot defeat. Nick Faldo was so embarrassed by his victory that, after sinking his winning putt, he gave Norman a long hug and said, "I feel horrible about what happened. I'm so sorry."[141]

The phenomenon is by no means confined to golf though. In basketball it is "the bricks", whilst others may know it as "bottling" or simply "choking". It appears just at the time when we least want it, as we stand poised on the cusp of achieving our dream. Whether putting to win the US Masters golf tournament, serving to win Wimbledon, taking a penalty in the European Cup Final or even giving an important presentation at work, in any situation where we desperately want to succeed, the yips are lurking. In football, it seems to afflict penalty-takers especially, for otherwise it is difficult to account for seasoned professionals missing the goal altogether from a distance of 12 yards. Excruciating examples abound. In the 1994 World Cup, Roberto Baggio, having been the best player in the tournament up to that point, contrived to blast the ball well over the bar in the penalty shoot-out, thereby handing the trophy to Brazil. John Terry, desperate to crown his Chelsea career by winning the European Cup, slipped and saw his spot-kick hit the post in the penalty shoot-out at the end of the 2008 final. And Lionel Messi, arguably the best footballer ever, was so upset by the penalty he blazed over the bar for Argentina in the 2016 Copa America final, that he immediately announced his retirement from international football (although he changed his mind a couple of months later).

British table-tennis champion Matthew Syed recounts his own personal experience in his book *Bounce*. He had spent months preparing for the 2000 Sydney Olympic Games. Nothing had been left to chance. He had had sessions with psychologists, nutritionists and physiologists. Once in Australia, two international players had been especially flown in so that he could practise with them, and the club where they played even reproduced the flooring that would be used in the Olympic competition hall. At the age of 29, Matthew was probably at his last Olympics, but was in with a realistic hope of reaching the medal stages. And then came his first match. As he tells it:

Franz stroked the ball into play – a light and gentle tophand forespin. It was not a difficult stroke to return, not a stroke I would normally have had any trouble pouncing upon, and yet I was strangely late on it, my feet stuck in their original position, my racket jabbing at the ball in a way that was totally unfamiliar. My return missed the table by more than two feet.[142]

Things went from bad to worse. As he goes on, "My movements were sometimes lethargic, sometimes jerky, my technique lacking any semblance of fluency and coherence." Matthew lost 21-8, 21-4, a completely humiliating defeat. As his coach helpfully pointed out to him afterwards, "You choked."[143]

Work and romance are other areas where we may find ourselves under particular pressure. Giving a vital sales pitch on behalf of his team as part of the UK *Apprentice* TV show in 2014, one of the contestants, Mark Wright, although well-used to public speaking, found himself unable to get out a coherent sentence. As he said afterwards, "I wanted to do a good job so badly that I let that overwhelm me."[144] Alan Sugar forgave him his blip though, and he went on to win the series. And a truly sad, but perhaps perfect definition of choking in romance is given by a Professor of Organisational Behaviour (who presumably knows a bit about how to talk to people), Declan Fitzsimons. At 52, and regretting that he hadn't had children, he reflected on a time when things might have gone down a different path, on "that evening six years ago when I managed in one short hour to say all the wrong things to the right woman, precisely because she was the right woman." To compound matters, a few days later the woman in question met someone else and went on to marry him.[145]

And it's not only sport, work and romance. In any situation where we are under extreme pressure to succeed we can be at risk of choking. It can afflict musicians, artists, surgeons and actors, in fact people from all walks of life. It could strike us when getting out our opening line on a first date or when launching into a wedding speech. It is a weird thing to observe, especially when it happens to a performer at the top of their game. As Matthew Syed puts it, "complex motor skills, built up over thousands of hours of practice, seem to vanish into the ether."[146]

I would suggest that choking can also be a collective experience. When England played Iceland in the last 16 of the European football championships in 2016, England were the overwhelming favourites. However, after going 2-1 behind, the England players went from bad to worse, playing misplaced pass after misplaced pass, overhitting free kicks and generally looking shadows of their normal selves. It looked like a collective case of choking, brought on by the knowledge that they had a relatively short time in which to redeem themselves in the match, failing which they would be humiliated. The short pass is perhaps the simplest action in football, forming the building block of the modern game, and yet professional footballers, who could almost do that in their sleep, became incapable of it as the pressure intensified. Fear of failure led to their downfall. Contrast this perhaps with Liverpool's fabled European Cup exploits in 2005. 3-0 down at half-time in the final against AC Milan, in the second half the team came out battling, fought their way back into the game, scored 3 goals in a six-minute spell, and won the game on penalties. This was a team with nothing to lose, and they became fearless, executing a game plan brilliantly. AC Milan by contrast seemed to have spent half-time celebrating their presumed victory and looked completely unable to cope with the second half turn of events.

But why does this sort of thing happen? There was certainly huge pressure on Greg Norman at the US Masters. He knew that the title was his to lose, and he also knew that he had been in similar positions before and had blown those leads. In contrast, Nick Faldo felt no pressure at all, and was so completely relaxed about the whole thing that on that final morning he became caught up watching motorsport on television and turned up at the course half an hour late. He just turned up and played his usual (excellent) round of golf, but Greg Norman seemed to have lost that ability completely. Faldo's coach, David Leadbetter, described Norman's technique on that day. "His routine is so different. He's standing over the ball an incredible amount of time. I'd say he's spending six, seven seconds longer per shot, fidgeting, moving around in ways I've never seen him do."

Sportspeople often say that the times that they perform best are when they are "in the zone". It is a wonderful state of mind, enabling them to play without thinking and allow their abilities to shine through. Tiger Woods has said that when he plays his best golf, it is as though "my body just takes over and I get out of my own way". Greg Norman's problem was that he just couldn't stop getting in his own way.

Tiger Woods' neat summary has been put in somewhat more technical language by Professor Russell Poldrack, a neuroscientist at Stanford University. He has said that, when we are learning a new skill, we use the prefrontal cortex of the brain, but when we have mastered it, control goes to other areas such as the basal ganglia, so that, instead of having to think about what we are doing, we act automatically.[147]

Imagine that you are learning to drive a car. For me this was a tortuous process, and such was the level of concentration required in using just the right amount of clutch, smoothly taking my foot off the accelerator and changing into gear, all the while looking at the road and steering, that I really didn't imagine how I would ever master it. And the thought of doing all that whilst simultaneously listening to the radio was completely ridiculous! However, eventually I got everything working together, and now that that skill has gone into the deeper parts of my brain, I change gear subconsciously as the need arises, without having to think about the process at all.

Ask a top tennis player how it was that they executed a particularly brilliant stroke and they won't be able to tell you. They have done it subconsciously, without thinking, their body automatically drawing on the hours and hours of practice. It is not possible for them to rationalise it because there are just too many interconnecting variables for the conscious mind to handle. If the conscious mind is allowed to have control, failure becomes inevitable.

The pressure that he was under meant that Greg Norman's access to the deeper parts of his brain was intermittent. The inbuilt technique that his years of practice had built up seemed to disappear, and thus, being forced to think his actions through, he was left dilly-dallying about before playing his shot.

It is cruelly ironic that top performers, having put themselves through endless practice to enable them to achieve great things, may find that, when it really matters, the incentive that drove them may be the very thing that stands in their way.

So what can be done to ward off this ghastly phenomenon? How can we "get out of our own way" as Tiger Woods put it, and achieve that fabled state of flow, where everything feels effortless? We need some mechanism for relieving the pressure, to convince ourselves that, as snooker World Champion Steve Davis has put it, we are "playing as if it means nothing when it means everything." Footballers may be exhorted to, "Just go out and enjoy yourselves," whilst British speed-skater Sarah Lindsay's technique was to repeat, "It's only speed-skating," to herself prior to her first-ever Olympic final in 2002. Many golfers have their own tried and tested methods. Some may concentrate on their breathing as they putt or, like the great Sam Snead, hum a tune to themselves to stop the conscious mind from interfering too much.[148] Taking a deep breath relaxes the body, and even a quick prayer has been shown to relieve stress, which perhaps is why we see so many footballers making the sign of the cross when taking to the pitch.

Sadly, my own footballing career only took me to the occasional heights of the third division of the Mid-Sussex League, representing the Hartfield 1st XI on those occasions when they were short of a ball-playing centre-back. However, even at that level there was a certain amount of pressure, and my own technique for dealing with it was to (albeit unknowingly) follow Sam Snead's example. Driving to matches I would play a tuneful piece of upbeat music (a particular favourite was XTC's *Senses Working Overtime*), with the aim of lodging it in my brain for the duration of the match, so that I didn't engage in too much over-analysis and was able to achieve at least a partial state of "flow".

Interestingly, some athletes seem not only to be able to not choke, but to actually perform better under intense pressure. We might think of Jonny Wilkinson who, with 26 seconds remaining in the 2003 Rugby World Cup Final, scored the winning drop goal against Australia, or of David Beckham who, deep into injury time in a vital 2001 football World Cup match, stepped up to drill a perfect free kick past the Greek goalkeeper. Analysis of some of these so-called "clutch performances" has revealed that these athletes adopted specific strategies to enable them to succeed. These included deliberately focussing on the task at hand, putting in intense effort and not thinking about the consequences of failure.[149] And indeed, when I look back at my own modest (well, very modest) achievements on the athletics track, I can see that I managed to pull off the occasional clutch performance. My breakthrough came in my last year at school in the final of the 800 metres. Athletically, I had always been the bridesmaid, but this time I was determined that things would be different. I reasoned that, if I tucked in behind the leading runner and then surprised everyone by making a break 300 metres from home, I would give myself the chance of upsetting the odds. I followed the plan to the letter, put a lot of effort in and, much to my amazement, it all worked perfectly, giving me a wholly unexpected victory! Ah, the joy of a clutch performance.

One of the lovely things about modern life is that we have so much choice in so many areas. Whereas a couple of hundred years ago our potential life partner would have been someone living close to us, with the advent of easy travel, Tinder, Facebook and Internet dating agencies catering for every possible proclivity (including Cat Lovers Dating, Clown Dating (because "it's no fun looking for love when you're a clown"), Gluten Free Singles, Muddymatches.co.uk (for "farmers who want a wife"), Tall Singles, Shortersingles.co.uk, and at least 4 websites for lovelorn Trekkies[150]), there are now millions of possibilities.

However, despite all of these apparent opportunities, I am sure that all of us will have friends who are desperate to find the "right" person. But it may be that the sheer range of possibilities is actually hindering their quest.

In so many areas of life we have moved on from a Hobson's choice situation, of being forced to accept whatever we are offered. When I buy my apples, I like to be able to pick the freshest and juiciest myself. However, being faced with too much choice can bring its own challenges. I am very keen on records, and sifting through a box of vinyl is a fine way to while some time away. However, I have on occasion walked into a whole warehouse full of boxes of records and the sight has caused my heart to sink. Part of me is keen to get on and see what gems lie within, whilst another part is filled with horror at the thought that I will only ever be able to look through a tiny fraction. An hour or two's searching is quite enough for me, but even a couple of days would be insufficient for this lot. So, as likely as not, I will listlessly flick through a few, but if nothing interesting leaps out, I will call it a day. Paradoxically, if there were only half a dozen or so boxes, I would search through them all diligently, but, in the face of too much choice, what should be a joy just becomes a chore.

If the thought of hunting through old records does not appeal, imagine rather that you are in a beautiful restaurant and have been seated at an elegant table. You order your drinks and are brought the menu. But it is simply huge – the size of a telephone directory, and includes just about every dish imaginable. You eagerly open it and begin to leaf through, marvelling at the delights on offer. However, with each appearing more exotic and delicious sounding than the last, you soon find yourself overwhelmed by the extent of the offerings. Although you initially analyse the courses carefully, as you progress, you steadily read faster and faster, until finally you just flick from page to page.* When the waitress returns, exhaustedly you leave the menu unopened on the table and ask her what she would recommend. Whilst we appreciate having a choice of meals, having too many to choose from is a burden.

Deborah Orr, writing about television programmes in *The Guardian*, encapsulated this problem when she lamented that, "The huge selection that's available, watchable whenever one feels like it, has actually contracted my viewing habits."[151] And John Kay, reviewing Renata Salecl's book *Choice*, notes that whilst in France, he visited Maison Herbin, an artisanal producer of delicious jams. However, being faced with over a hundred jams from which to choose, it all became a bit much for him. He managed to narrow his selection down to about thirty, but in the end the effort was so great that he left without any jam at all.[152]

This outcome would have come as no surprise to Sheena Iyengar, a social psychologist at Columbia University, and Mark Lepper, a psychologist at Stanford, who in 2002, set up their own choice experiment involving exotic jam. They set up a tasting stall in an upmarket grocers, but at different times of day made either 6 or 24 varieties available. When there was a choice of 24, more people stopped to try (60%, compared with 40% for the 6 jam selection), but when it came to actually buying a jar, it was a different matter. Even though everyone who stopped was given a discount voucher, only 4 out of the 145 people who stopped at the table with the 24 jams on display went on to make a purchase, whilst 31 of the 104 people who stopped at the 6 jam selection bought a jar.[153]

It has been argued that this result defies logic, as supermarkets offer an enormous range of groceries. As it happens, peanut butter and marmalade sandwiches have long been a particular favourite of mine, and my local Sainsbury's offers me a choice of 43 different jars of peanut (or similar) butters. (The marmalade has been supplied for many years by my mother, and Sainsbury's aren't going to come up with anything to compete with that.) So, if customers are befuddled by choice, why don't the supermarkets, with all their sophisticated research techniques, limit the varieties available to about 6? However, I think that the two examples are actually very different. Those who passed by the researchers' tables probably did not set out that morning with the intention of buying a jar of exotic jam, and would be choosing a jar because it was both unusual and sounded tasty. When I visit the supermarket, I have already done my choosing and have my list to hand to speed me on my way. If the brand of peanut butter that I want is available at about a price that I am expecting, I will buy it and not agonise over the alternatives. However, a few weeks back, when I went to Sainsbury's to buy some peanut butter, I discovered that my brand of choice was on special offer, with the consequence that it had sold out. I then had to spend quite some time agonising over the alternatives in an attempt to find the precise compromise between price and quality that would leave me least dissatisfied.

Because so many customers have their own particular choice of brands, if supermarkets fail to offer each customer their favourite, they will be tempted to go elsewhere to buy it (and quite possibly other groceries) rather than accepting one of the alternatives. This thinking has led American supermarkets to increase the number of products available in an average store from 8,948 in 1975 to almost 47,000 in 2008,[154] although we may now have reached peak choice, as in 2015 Tesco actually began to cut back on the number of different varieties stocked in its UK stores. At the time, its 90,000 different items included a choice of 228 different air fresheners, ranging from its basic own-label to varieties that had an integral fan or came disguised as stones,[155] so it is possible to see that there might be scope for rationalisation.

Choice, of course, is not limited to supermarkets. Under the American healthcare system, patients are provided with a complete list of alternative treatments and treatment providers, including details of possible likely outcomes, cost and side effects. Often there will be 20 to 30 to choose between, and, when drug plan options are added, there can be as many as 50 possibilities from which to choose. But as we have seen, when faced with too many choices, people lose the will to evaluate them all properly. As Brian Elbel, Assistant Professor of Medicine and Health Policy at New York University, has observed, many people become overwhelmed when faced with all of these healthcare options and so do not make the best choices.[156] Studies on choice have been conducted covering everything from boxes of chocolate to restaurant wine lists, indicating that we actually choose more wisely when faced with a smaller range of choices, with the optimum number seeming to be about half a dozen. Once there are many more than that, people are much more likely to choose the default option (which in a restaurant would probably mean opting for today's "special" or asking the waiter what they recommended) or even deciding not to choose, perhaps putting the decision off to a later time. Even in the realm of speed dating, where the whole ethos is to maximise choice, the very range of options that potential suitors are presented with tends to make their actual choices poorer. A review of psychological studies[157] suggested that when faced with more choice than we can comfortably handle, we focus more on superficial qualities (i.e. looks) than on characteristics that are actually more valuable in a long-term relationship. Having too much choice is not in our best interests,[158] but that is just what we are faced with. Eric Beinhocker of the Institute for New Economic Thinking has estimated that, in New York City, consumers are presented with a staggering 10 billion choices every day.[159] We clearly need to find a way to navigate that maze without sending ourselves mad, but the methods that we use do not always result in the best outcome.

A classic example is the hypothetical case of the two very similar restaurants which sit opposite each other in a tourist area. At the beginning of the evening they are both empty. Then the first couple of tourists come along looking for somewhere to eat and, more or less at random, pick one of the restaurants. The next couple, seeing that one restaurant is apparently more popular than the other, make the same choice, and so it goes, so that by mid-evening, one restaurant has a queue out of the door, whilst the other remains empty. Our choice mechanism has led to inefficiencies, chefs in one restaurant being worked to death whilst others stand around with nothing to do, and in the end, the possibility that a restaurant could go out of business just because of the random choice of a couple of tourists. Indeed, whilst holidaying in America, my wife and I were staying in Boston and found ourselves with a choice of two possible venues for breakfast. Perhaps inevitably, we picked the one with a queue out of the door rather than the one that was completely empty. To be fair, the empty one, with its white starched tablecloths, did look unnecessarily posh (and expensive) for breakfast, but even so, it would have taken a degree of effort (which I did not feel myself capable of first thing in the morning) to be the first across the threshold. This type of self-reinforcing behaviour drives inequalities in all sorts of areas, so that once something achieves a degree of popularity, it gathers momentum simply because of that.**

So how do we cope with all this choice? Very often, some ordering will have been imposed. Thus, when I go into a supermarket, happily, all the peanut butter is gathered together in one place, rather than being scattered randomly throughout the store. A typical restaurant menu, rather than presenting a single list of, say, 30 possible choices, will break them down into categories such as meat, fish, pasta and rice, so enabling the diner to make an initial selection between half a dozen or so types of food, before then considering the specific meal that they would like.

Another solution may be found by utilising the power of the list. I have recently been trying to find a nice holiday cottage in Shropshire. The Internet has made this sort of search far more daunting. In the past, the prospective holidaymaker would probably have sent away for a few brochures, flicked through the pages to select the most appropriate and booked it. Now, however, given the massive expansion of possibilities, there is increased pressure to find the very best possible cottage, combining all aspects of value, location, facilities, old (or new) world charm, views, parking etc. Some even up the ante by offering to deliver home-cooked meals to your door every evening. The fear is that you have never quite checked every one, so there remains the possibility that there exists one that is a little nearer to your preferred location, with a slightly more luxurious bathroom or better view from the upstairs balcony. All of which may mean that you are trying to choose between a dozen different cottages, none of which is absolutely perfect, and suspecting that if you only go on looking, your ideal cottage will appear. It is at this stage that a website such as TripAdvisor comes into its own. You set your parameters and the site will produce for you a list of say 70 suitable cottages, but a list that is in order of popularity. Not only has your potentially endless search now been reduced to 70, but because they are in order, you can start at the top, go through perhaps the first ten, and choose the best of those, secure in the belief that they will only get worse from there. This popularity of such sites reflects the understanding of psychologists Claude Messner and Michaela Wänke who, in 2011, concluded that the faster we decide on something, and the less effort the decision-making process is, the happier we are.[160]

Thus, if I find myself in a large second-hand record shop, I impose procedures that will limit my options. I give myself a time limit (or find that one is imposed on me by my fellow shopper) and select a particular area to begin. Even though I know that the best treasures are to be found in the awkwardly placed boxes on the ground, I am of an age where I forego these in the interests of my knees. Ideally, the shop will have done some sorting into categories, so I refer to a list on my phone to remind myself of records that I am particularly keen to find (perhaps the second album by the Beat or an obscure House of Love 12"), and go from there.

Daily Telegraph cookery writer Diana Henry has faced up to the problem of choice when trying to make decisions with her children. She found that if she offers them too many food options, her "ten-year-old's eyes will glaze over, and he will ask for his staple (pasta, tuna and sweetcorn)." And the family's Friday night time together can be ruined by the effort involved in choosing between all that is available on Netflix, DVD, TV or iPlayer, so she now assesses the options beforehand and for meals and viewing presents a choice of just three.[161]

In everyday life we can make things easier for ourselves by setting default options or rules for everyday activities. We may opt to have a default sandwich option, such as the aforementioned peanut butter and marmalade (truly the queen of sandwich fillings), elect to go for a healthy run at one specified time each week, or always aim for a certain place in our regular car park.****

Spotify users will be familiar with the extraordinary choice of music that it offers to listeners. By typing the name of an artist or song into its search function, music fans can be listening within seconds to any one of over 35 million tracks. However, Spotify has not been very inspiring if you don't know quite what you fancy listening to, and it is extremely intimidating being faced with the equivalent of the biggest record shop imaginable, stuffed with racks of CDs from floor to ceiling and being asked to choose something to listen to. To help listeners cope with all this choice, Spotify has been moving from the "search" model, where the user has to do the work, to a "discovery" model, helping the listener to find new music that they might like, based on their prior listening habits and its recommended playlists.[162]

Government agencies too have sometimes attempted to resolve some of the downsides of too much choice, but sadly, these efforts are not always successful. One ongoing issue in the UK concerned the high cost of power. One of the problems was that energy companies offered households so many different tariffs that it became exceedingly difficult for customers to tell which was the best for them. Indeed, in 2012 the consumer organisation Which? claimed to have found over 1,440 different tariffs.[163] The price paid may be dependent on whether your account is online, where you live, whether the price is fixed, and if so, for how long, when the deal was launched and how you pay. This tactic, understandably known as "confusion marketing", makes it so hard to find the best deal that many consumers do not even bother to try. In the same year, the UK energy regulator Ofgem took action to force the companies to simplify their tariffs. However, even this backfired, with companies tending to axe their cheapest deals and doing away with special offers for the vulnerable, thus actually increasing costs to many consumers.[164]

So, hopefully we are now armed with strategies to enable us to cope with too much pressure and too much choice, but of course there are other ways of smacking ourselves in the face, as the case of Barbra Streisand's house has very neatly illustrated.

Barbra's problem began in 2002, when the California Coastal Records Project set out to document erosion along the California coastline. They engaged photographer Kenneth Adelman to take more than 12,000 photos along the coast, one of which happened to include Barbra's cliff-top property. Along with the others, this photograph was posted on the Project's website, where it sat for a short period until the Project received a cease-and-desist letter from Ms Streisand's lawyers. This was followed in short order by a US$50 million lawsuit against the photographer and the hosting websites. In December 2003 a court ruled that the photograph was not in fact an infringement of privacy, but the lawsuit had attracted a huge amount of publicity, resulting in 420,000 people visiting the Project's website just to view the photo of Barbra's house. It subsequently transpired that, prior to issuing the lawsuit, the photo had been accessed 6 times, of which 2 were by her own lawyers. This type of unintended consequence has quite rightly become known as the "Streisand Effect" in her honour.

Ten years later, another singer, this time Beyoncé, discovered the power of the Streisand Effect for herself. She had sung and danced her heart out during the half-time interval of the 2013 American Super Bowl, a performance that was widely acclaimed. Not least by BuzzFeed website, which published 33 photos which they claimed showed Beyoncé at her "fiercest". However, Beyoncé's PR firm Shure Media took a different view of the photos, and wrote to the website politely commenting that, "there are some unflattering photos on your current feed that we are respectfully asking you to change." Unfortunately, the website published the email, alongside the seven pictures that the PR had identified as being "the worst", resulting in the dispute being picked up by media around the world, who blazoned the supposedly unflattering photos to a much wider audience.[165]

In 2014, irascible UK indie band The Fall had something that they also wished to have covered up, but in their case it was an album that a record company had released, against their wishes, for the annual UK Record Store Day. They voiced their opinion in no uncertain terms on their website, ending with the allegation that, "What they are doing is illegal and is fraud." The record company went ahead anyway and the release became an (albeit somewhat limited) beneficiary of the Streisand Effect, with orders of almost twice those expected. As the sales manager wryly wrote, "We must remember to thank The Fall for mentioning our RSD release on their website... There's no such thing as bad advertising."

One might think that a way of avoiding the Streisand Effect would be to apply a so-called "super-injunction" to the delicate matter in question. These are fearsome legal powers intended not only to suppress a story but to forbid any mention even of the existence of the injunction. Such was the theory of lawyers acting on behalf of footballer Ryan Giggs who, in May 2011, became aware that a forthcoming book by former "Big Brother" contestant Imogen Thomas was to reveal that she had had an affair with the apparently happily married footballer. They accordingly obtained a super-injunction, but this caused great offence amongst the British news media and an outbreak of thinly veiled hints, until eventually his name was revealed via Twitter. However, the lawyers, as they seem prone to do, ploughed on, and unsuccessfully attempted to sue Twitter, resulting in over 75,000 Twitter users outing Giggs as the adulterer. Such was the furore that the matter was raised in Parliament, where MP John Hemming used Parliamentary privilege to name Giggs without fear of prosecution, thus giving the whole story further exposure. However, according to Ms Thomas' publicist Max Clifford, she had never intended to reveal the affair in her book, and as he said, "If he hadn't taken out a super-injunction, no one would probably have known about this relationship."[166]**** If that were indeed the case, Mr Giggs had gone to a great deal of effort, only to shine a spotlight on that which he wished to remain hidden.

Ryan Giggs' lawyers might have benefited from knowing when to stop, as failure to do so seems to be a sure-fire way of encouraging unintended consequences. Such was the case in 2014, when a minor dispute between a hairdresser and his customer escalated out of all proportion. Janice Khoo had gone to her hairdresser, Drew Carlton, for hair extensions, which had cost £360 (about US$470). However, she immediately complained that he had made her look as though she had just got out of bed. After Mr Carlton ordered her out of the shop, she left an unfavourable comment online, to which Mr Carlton responded by posting a string of barely coherent rants on his company's Facebook page. Amongst other (unrepeatable) things, he claimed that Mrs Khoo had a "histrionic personality disorder you old insecure witch!!" As a result, Mrs Khoo understandably claimed to be traumatised, reported the matter to the police and it was picked up by the national press, all of which did little to enhance the salon's reputation. As Mr Carlton later admitted, "I wanted to protect my business. I realise now that probably did more harm."[167]

A more serious result of overreacting came about in the aftermath of the so-called "Baby P" case in 2007. 17-month-old Peter Connelly (referred to in court as "Baby P") died horribly at the hands of his mother, her boyfriend and her boyfriend's brother after suffering months of cruelty. There was a huge outcry, and the media focused its attention on the baby's social worker, Maria Ward, and the director of children's services, Sharon Shoesmith. They were vilified, and protesters and politicians called for action. Rebekah Brooks, then editor of the *Sun* newspaper, went to the lengths of setting up a petition calling for Sharon Shoesmith to be fired, which duly happened shortly after, live on television.***** And what was the consequence of this furore? Did social services improve as a result? On the contrary, social workers left the profession in droves, leaving those who remained with greater caseloads and consequently less time to spend on each case. The increase in workload was exacerbated by the fear of being seen to fail to protect any child in their care, which led social workers to adopt a "no-risk" approach, and so thousands more children were taken into care each year. As the put-upon cartoon character Dilbert observed about increases in his own workload, "I have infinite capacity to do more work, as long as you don't mind that my quality approaches zero." Tragically, the effect on child safety turned out to the opposite of what everybody wanted. In the year following the outcry, the number of children killed by their parents in the United Kingdom increased by more than 25%, and the figure remained higher for the next three years. Pointing the finger of blame in the wake of the tragic death of Peter Connelly was an unmitigated disaster.

However, whilst it is perhaps understandable to react in this way, other professions have managed to avoid playing the blame game when errors are made. The air industry is particularly good at this. In the 1940s there was a spate of crashes of B-17 bombers, all caused by the pilot pressing the wrong switch as the planes came in to land. Instead lifting the wing-flaps, they were lifting the landing gear. The pilots were well trained and shouldn't have made that mistake. However, rather than vilifying the dead pilots and exhorting the rest to do better, an investigation was launched to try to find out exactly why they were making the mistake. The problem turned out to be that, because the switches were right next to each other and looked identical, it was all too easy to flick the wrong one. So a small wheel was attached to the landing-gear switch and a flap shape to the flaps control. This kind of accident stopped immediately.[168]

In the corporate world, as in social services, there is a tendency to point the finger of responsibility straight at individuals. However, here it is not so much seeking to blame, but rather to motivate. In their quest for ever higher profits, companies have sought to incentivise staff in positions of responsibility by offering them ever bigger bonuses. The argument usually put forward for such rewards is that the bonus element motivates the recipient to deliver better returns for the company. However, research going back over 100 years suggests that offering extreme rewards for success can actually reduce performance below the levels achieved when much smaller rewards are offered. In one 2009 Indian experiment, participants were rewarded with prizes of 4, 40 or 400 rupees (400 rupees being about an average monthly wage for the participants) for "very good" performance in a variety of challenging games. There were six games in all between them designed to test creativity, memory and physical dexterity. The memory games included "Simon" and "Recall last 3 digits" and the physical capability tests included balancing a ball around a labyrinth and "Roll Up", a game that requires participants to deftly roll a ball along two rods. In one game the participants were given nine metal quarter circles and asked to arrange them so that they fitted into a frame. If they did it within 4 minutes, they received half of the possible reward, but if they managed it within 2 minutes, they scooped the full amount. Of those offered the smallest reward, 29% managed it inside 4 minutes and 25% inside 2 minutes. Those offered the medium reward did slightly better, with 43% achieving it within 4 minutes and 33% within 2. However, for those who had a whole month's wages hanging on the result, the pressure of the possible reward had a terrible effect, with only 10% of them finishing within 4 minutes, whilst not one of them managed it within 2 minutes. In none of the games did those offered the highest reward perform best.

The authors suggested a couple of particular reasons why this might be so. Firstly, when presented with the promise of an extreme reward for accomplishing a particular task, as we have seen in the sporting world, there is the tendency to "choke" and, when a huge bonus is a possibility, the mind of the recipient naturally tends to focus on the bonus itself and its consequences for their life, rather than on the task that they actually need to perform in order to gain the reward.[169]

In another study, carried out in the 1970s, Stanford's Mark Lepper and his colleagues invited participants to play some games just for fun. They then introduced a system giving rewards for success. However, when they took the rewards away again, the participants found that they no longer derived enjoyment just from playing, and that the introduction of the reward had changed what had been a fun game into work. By bringing an incentive structure into people's work, the intrinsic satisfaction that they find in that work can be lost, so that they come to feel that they are just working for the reward. Their motivation becomes the reward itself, rather than the job, and so there is a strong temptation to cut corners or attempt to game the system in order to ensure that the reward is achieved. Even for those not tempted, the tendency is that the reward will prove to be an unhelpful distraction.

In 1993, author Alfie Kohn wrote in the *Harvard Business Review* that:

As for productivity, at least two dozen studies over the last three decades have conclusively shown that people who expect to receive a reward for completing a task or for doing that task successfully simply do not perform as well as those who expect no reward at all. These studies examined rewards for children and adults, males and females, and included tasks ranging from memorizing facts to creative problem-solving to designing collages. In general, the more cognitive sophistication and open-ended thinking that was required, the worse people performed when working for a reward.[170]

However, any lessons learned from such research have largely been ignored. Researchers Brian Hall of Harvard Business School and Kevin Murphy of the University of Southern California found that, in the decade prior to 2003, the amount of total executive compensation which was contingent on share price had risen from 10% to almost 70%.[171]

To give just a very few examples of the sort of amounts being paid in the banking sector, in 2008, as their banks were being driven on to the rocks, Bob Diamond, chief executive of

Barclays Capital Investment Bank, took a bonus of £6.5 million (about US$8.5 million), Fred Goodwin, chief executive of RBS, was paid a bonus of £2.86 million (about US$3.7 million) and Peter Cummings, head of corporate lending at HBOS, received a £1.8 million (about US$2.3 million) bonus. And these were extras, on top of their already generous basic pay. The cost to the British taxpayer of the disaster that ensued in the crash was almost unimaginably massive. Billions of pounds were supplied in loans and guarantees to Barclays, £20 billion (about US$26 billion) was used to prop up RBS, whilst HBOS had to be rescued by Lloyds Bank, with the combined bank being supported by another £20 billion of government money. By the end of 2010, the total amount of money poured into banks by the UK Government was £124 billion (about US$161 billion), whilst the taxpayer's possible liability was £512 billion (about US$666 billion), just £10 billion (about US$1.6 billion) short of the UK Government's entire annual income. As we have seen, the bonus system was by no means the sole cause of the 2008 crash but, as the 2009 Turner Review, carried out for the UK's Financial Services Authority, concluded, there was a "strong prima facie case that inappropriate incentive structures played a role in encouraging behaviour which contributed to the financial crisis" and that it is likely that remuneration policies "have created incentives for some executives and traders to take excessive risks and have resulted in large payments in reward for activities which seemed profit-making at the time but subsequently proved harmful to the institution, and in some cases *to the entire system*"[172] (my italics).

Tim Harford, writing in the *Financial Times*, summed up the problem and possible solution thus:

The basic principle for any incentive scheme is this: can you measure everything that matters? If you can't, then high-powered financial incentives will simply produce short-sightedness, narrow-

mindedness or outright fraud. If a job is complex, multifaceted and involves subtle trade-offs, the best approach is to hire good people, pay them the going rate and tell them to do the job to the best of their ability.[173]

One would like to think that the crash might have been the bucket of cold water that brought the industry to its senses, but the bonuses bounced straight back, with the top 1,265 staff in the 8 leading London banks receiving an average bonus of £1.8 million (about US$2.3 million) in 2010.[174] However, it is possible that the message may at last be getting through. In 2016 the founders of Woodford Investment Management, one of the UK's most respected and profitable investment funds, said that they would stop paying bonuses altogether, their justification being that:

There is little correlation between bonus and performance and this is backed by widespread academic evidence. Many studies conclude that bonuses don't work as a motivator, as expectation is already built in. Behavioural studies also suggest that bonuses can lead to short-term decision making and wrong behaviours.[175]

Incentives are of course not limited to the world of high finance. Many parents will be only too aware of their lure and potential danger. I know of one mother who, in attempting to potty train her toddler, offered him a toy car as an incentive. However, he seemed to cotton on pretty quickly to the possibilities and managed to string things along for some time. By the time he finally gave in, he had also managed to secure a toy bear, a book, some building bricks and a rucksack to put them all in. His parents were careful not to repeat the experiment with their subsequent children.

Other rewards offered by parents can have their own downsides. Many will offer incentives for passing important exams, but even if they appear to achieve their short-term objective, they can leave the student concentrating more on the reward than on the intrinsic benefits of study, give the message that satisfaction in the achievement itself is insufficient, and foster materialism in adulthood, which itself can lead on to compulsive purchasing, gambling and financial problems.[176]

If we are able to find satisfaction in the job itself, external rewards become unnecessary. We often hear of people landing their "dream job" and saying that they would have happily done it for nothing.

Tom Sawyer took a slightly different slant to a similar problem. Forced by his Aunt Polly to spend the afternoon whitewashing a fence, and having had his offer of payment in the form of a white marble spurned by his friend Jim, he has the following conversation with another passer-by, Ben:

> "Why, it's you, Ben! I warn't noticing."
>
> "Say – I'm going in a-swimming, I am. Don't you wish you could? But of course you'd druther work – wouldn't you? Course you would!"
>
> Tom contemplated the boy a bit, and said: "What do you call work?"
>
> "Why, ain't that work?"
>
> Tom resumed his whitewashing, and answered carelessly:
>
> "Well, maybe it is, and maybe it ain't. All I know, is, it suits Tom Sawyer."
>
> "Oh come, now, you don't mean to let on that you like it?"
>
> The brush continued to move.
>
> "Like it? Well, I don't see why I oughtn't to like it. Does a boy get a chance to whitewash a fence every day?"
>
> That put the thing in a new light.[177]

Ben and other boys become convinced by this argument and join in to help, so that, by suggesting to his friends that there are intrinsic benefits to white-washing, the fence finishes up with three coats and Tom has had a pleasant afternoon. As Mark Twain goes on to observe:

> *If he had been a great and wise philosopher, like the writer of this book, he would now have comprehended that Work consists of whatever a body is obliged to do, and that Play consists of whatever a body is not obliged to do. And this would help him to understand why constructing artificial flowers or performing on a tread-mill is work, while rolling ten-pins or climbing Mont Blanc is only amusement. There are wealthy gentlemen in England who drive four-horse passenger-coaches twenty or thirty miles on a daily line, in the summer, because the privilege costs them considerable money; but if they were offered wages for the service, that would turn it into work and then they would resign.*[178]

I discovered the truth of this for myself whilst in my teens, when for a couple of years my summer holiday was to go and help refurbish a Family Centre in the East End of London, paying for the privilege. And yet, working with and getting to know other people, those two holidays were amongst the best I've had, increased my self-confidence and led to a number of lasting friendships. No bonuses were on offer, but the intrinsic rewards were huge.

Too much pressure, too much choice and the wrong sort of incentives can all lead to us screwing-up that which we are most keen to achieve, but by making ourselves aware of the dangers, we have taken the first step towards avoiding them. Perhaps every so often we might take a look at the way we approach things in our personal and professional lives, and see whether unintended consequences might be getting in the way of achieving our goals. The fact that something has always been done one way doesn't mean that it might not be worthwhile considering whether a different, even counter-intuitive approach might result in better outcomes.

* This of course is why so many companies competing in a crowded marketplace will call themselves "ABC Cars", "A-B Cars", "Alpha Car Hire" or the like. They know that we are unlikely to bother looking as far as "Your Car Hire". And having a surname starting with a "W" doesn't help with book sales.

** My vegan brother Dixe tells me that he often finds it difficult being in vegan restaurants simply because he's not used to having a choice at all. His fear of not choosing the tastiest dish brings with it a pressure he almost never experiences in ordinary restaurants. He says that, "I often joke when eating with omnivore friends in ordinary establishments that I've been spared 'the tyranny of choice' but it is actually true."

*** My wife dreads the occasions when I have to park in an unfamiliar, almost empty, car park. In order to ensure that I find the absolutely most convenient spot, I tend to drive round a few times, checking all the possibilities and generally using up any time that might have been saved.

**** Max Clifford's career came to a grinding halt in May 2014 when he was jailed for 8 years for carrying out indecent assaults on girls and young women.

***** Sharon Shoesmith subsequently won a claim against Haringey Council for unfair dismissal, with the judge saying that she had been "summarily scapegoated".[359]

Chapter 4

"Ouch!" – Why did that backfire?

Let us imagine ourselves transported back to a time when the Roman Empire ruled the known world, its armies sent to its furthest borders using a magnificent network of roads constructed by its engineers. A network which, even 2,000 years later, still provides the basis for many of Europe's main roads. The benefits of being able to dispatch an army along wide level highways, rather than rough cross-country tracks, is obvious. According to the Roman historian Vegetius, Roman soldiers were capable of marching along these roads, carrying their equipment, for up to 18 miles a day, with the milestones that they set up along the route enabling them to know exactly where they were. But roads are militarily neutral, and care not whether Roman soldiers or their enemies use them. And so, when in 60CE she led a revolt against the Romans, Boudicca, Queen of the Iceni, was able, with her 100,000 strong army, to speed along Roman roads from Camulodunum (now Colchester) to London and then back up to Verulamium (now St Albans), burning and killing as she went. Such was their speed that Roman London was caught unprepared and was burnt to the ground. So intense was the destruction that, if you were to dig far enough down in certain parts of modern-day London, you would find a layer of red ash, up to ten inches thick, marking the venting of Boudicca's wrath.

Although the burning of London came about through Roman technology backfiring, disasters can also occur even when both sides are well-intentioned. In fact, misunderstandings in international relations go back even further than the Romans. Nine hundred years earlier, David, king of Israel, learned of the death of the king of his neighbours, the Ammonites, and sent a delegation to express his sympathies. However, the Ammonites, being somewhat paranoid, assumed that this was part of a plot to spy out the city and overthrow them. David's party was, in the tradition of the time, wonderfully bearded, and in order to show their contempt for them, the Ammonite authorities arrested the visitors and shaved off one side of each man's beard and cut off their clothes at buttock level. The affront to Israel left King David with no alternative but to attack the Ammonites. The Ammonites raised a huge army of over 30,000 men but, after a year of war, they were defeated by David, their cities plundered and the inhabitants slaughtered. And all because David had tried to express his condolences.[179]

Blowback has continued to be a problem throughout history. Over a hundred years ago, the whole island of Ireland was part of the United Kingdom, and the British Government was exploring ways of giving it a degree of independence. Many in Ireland opposed this policy, and a group called the Ulster Volunteer Force got together to take whatever action it could to prevent this happening. By the end of 1913 they had over 90,000 members. The German Government, following the principle that "my enemy's enemy is my friend", smuggled 35,000 rifles to them in a bid to inflame matters. However, within a year the First World War had broken out, and the UVF "to a man"[180] signed up to the British Army to fight *against* the Germans, many of them bringing with them the guns that the Germans had so helpfully provided.

The Americans fell foul of the same policy mistake in Afghanistan decades later. In 1973, the Soviet Union supported Prince Mohammad Daoud as he overthrew the Afghan king and established a communist government. As the Germans had done in Ireland, the CIA began supporting their enemy's opposition, in this case groups of Islamic extremists. Such was the success of the resistance that in 1979 the Soviets were forced to invade the country in order to stop the Government falling.

With the Cold War going through a particularly frosty period, the US upped the ante, pouring US$3 billion into the region to support what it viewed as its plucky friends. Of this money, about half ended up in the coffers of the fundamentalist and totally ruthless mujaheddin leader Gulbuddin Hekmatyar.[181] His ruthlessness was especially appealing to the Americans, who were keen to see it applied to the Russians. Hekmatyar and other mujaheddin weren't totally reliant on the Americans though, and also raised a huge amount of money through drug trafficking, so that Afghan opium production increased from 250 tons in 1982 to 2,000 tons in 1991, to which the US turned a blind eye. By the late 1980s the CIA was also assisting another Islamist extremist, Osama bin Laden, through a mujaheddin front organisation called MAK.[182] With its main office in Brooklyn, New York, it funnelled money, arms and fighters from the outside world into Afghanistan,[183] and became the main conduit through which the CIA conducted its undercover war against the Russians there. The CIA threw more and more effort and resources into training and funding the Afghan jihadists, so that by the end of February 1989 the Soviets were forced to withdraw, although the Marxist Afghan Government struggled on for another 3 years.[184]

However, having won the war in Afghanistan, the Afghan fighters turned their attention elsewhere. This became clear in February 1993, when an audacious attempt was made to blow up New York's World Trade Center. A truck bomb was exploded in a car park underneath one of the Twin Towers, with the intention that one tower would be toppled, bringing the other down with it. The bomb failed in its objective but killed 6 people. It transpired that most of the bombers were associated with Gulbuddin Hekmatyar and had used CIA money to fund their training. The enemy of America's enemy had shown that it was America's enemy too, and as an internal CIA report concluded, "By giving these people the funding that we did, a situation was created in which it could be safely argued that we bombed the

World Trade Center."[185]

Things of course were to get much, much worse, as another man who had been financed and trained by the Americans, Osama bin Laden, successfully carried out Gulbuddin Hekmatyar's original plan when the Twin Towers of the World Trade Center were destroyed on 9/11. Almost 3,000 people were killed, an utterly appalling case of blowback.

Afghanistan is by no means the only place where Western involvement has backfired. In 2003 a Western alliance invaded Iraq with two primary objectives – to destroy Iraq's weapons of mass destruction and to remove Saddam Hussein from power. As it turned out, there were in fact no weapons of mass destruction to destroy, but Saddam Hussein was duly deposed. A Shiite-led Government replaced Hussein's Sunni-led Government, and the army (comprising mainly Sunni Muslims) was effectively disbanded, leaving about two hundred and fifty thousand men, "armed, angry and with military training... suddenly humiliated and out of work," as the *New Yorker* put it.[186] If that were not dangerous enough, when the Americans pulled out of Iraq in 2011, the Iraqi leader Nouri al-Maliki proceeded to repress the Sunnis ruthlessly, radicalising many of them in the process and effectively driving them into the arms of a new extremist organisation, which came to be called ISIS, and which had swept into the vacuum left by the Western powers.[187] As the then US President Barack Obama admitted in 2015, "ISIS is a direct outgrowth of al-Qaeda in Iraq that grew out of our invasion. It is an example of unintended consequences, which is why we should generally aim before we shoot."[188] Indeed, a study of the outcomes of the Iraq War, published in *Mother Jones* magazine in 2006, indicated that the War had global repercussions, having led to an increase in the number of worldwide terrorist attacks by 607% and consequent deaths by 237%.[189]

It is all too easy to find modern-day examples of blowback. For our third, we can look to Somalia, which by 2008 had become one of the most dangerous countries in the world. It had endured a 20-year civil war in which more than 400,000 people had died. The south of the country was dominated by al-Shabaab, a brutal militia linked to al-Qaeda. Pirate gangs were operating with apparent impunity, attacking and hijacking shipping as it passed along the Somali coast. It has been estimated that ransoms paid to the pirates in 2008 alone totalled upwards of US$50 million (about £38 million).

But how did this terrible situation arise? Al-Shabaab had originated as the military wing of the Islamic Courts Union, which had taken control of the capital, Mogadishu, in June 2006. Concerned by the way that things were going in Somalia, and keen to reduce the influence of al-Shabaab, the US Bush Administration secretly pressured Ethiopia to invade its neighbour, which it did in December 2006. However, although the ICU disintegrated almost immediately, the coup catapulted the extremists of al-Shabaab to the fore, as the opposition to the invaders coalesced around them. As Dr David Anderson, professor of African politics at Oxford University, said in 2011:

Western interventions have been well meaning but too often ill-informed and poorly executed. The US sponsored Ethiopian presence only worsened things; the Ethiopian presence giving radical groups a reason to gather support against foreign intervention. This strengthened al-Shabaab hugely and weakened the position of politicians, who the West hoped would rebuild political authority and re-establish the state. We are presently further from this outcome than ever.[190]

Looking back, it is shocking to see how often the presumption that "my enemy's enemy is my friend" has led the Americans to support organisations or regimes that have subsequently come back to bite them, including the financing of the Taliban in Afghanistan, Colonel Gaddafi in Libya and Saddam Hussein in Iraq. All too often these interventions seem to be undertaken without any coherent understanding of what the actual outcome might be. To repeat President Obama's words, it would be a much better idea if governments were to aim before they shoot. And as commentators John Hulsman and Lara Palay have said with respect to the West's involvement in Iraq, "Simply put, the West falls down at the first intellectual hurdle of analysis; we fail to put ourselves in others' shoes." They go on to quote TE Lawrence's advice that there is a way to avoid these nasty surprises, "experience of them (local peoples), and knowledge of their prejudices will enable you to foresee their attitude and possible course of action in nearly every case."[191] Time and again the West seeks to impose its own view of how the region should look, rather than recognising that Iraq actually breaks down into the ethno-religious groupings of Sunni, Shia and Kurds, and any "solution" which does not realise that is not going to secure any long-term success. When the Ottomans ruled Mesopotamia they divided the region into the three separate provinces of Basra, Baghdad and Mosul, respectively dominated by the Shia, Sunnis and Kurds. Hulsman and Palay conclude that, "Until we learn to stand in the shoes of the people of the region and analytically look at the world the way they do, we cannot hope to guess the decisions they will make, the help they will accept, the reforms they will adopt, the deals they will uphold – and the fears to which they will fall prey."[192]

Analysing the situation properly and aiming before we shoot are both very sensible precautions to take before embarking on any campaign. But for everyone concerned, it would be better still to avoid the necessity of any action. As Sun Tzu in his classic *The Art Of War* observed, what makes a general truly great is not their prowess in fighting, but their ability to achieve their objectives without resorting to war at all.[193] If the American Government had foreseen that passenger jets could be hijacked for use as flying bombs, they would have stepped up security before 9/11, so preventing that attack on the Twin Towers. The invasion of Afghanistan (and very likely the second Iraq invasion) would then have been unnecessary, and the lives of over 200,000 people[194] and more than US$1.7 trillion (about £1.3 trillion)[195] would have been saved.

One might have thought that with experience would come wisdom, and yet even a country such as Israel, well used to fighting its enemies almost continually since its formation in 1948, has failed to grasp the extent of the problem. A one-time head of Israeli security, Aharon Farkash, has mused that direct attacks on organisations such as Hezbollah, "Were forcing them to be more innovative... We forced them to evolve."[196] These attacks had the effect not of depleting the enemy's strength, but have acted somewhat like a vaccine, increasing their resilience. Hezbollah evolved from being a merely military organisation and began to integrate itself into Lebanese (and later Palestinian) society – rebuilding houses, sorting out everyday problems with plumbing and the like and becoming in effect a combination of local council and charitable organisation. As author Joshua Cooper Ramo has observed, "In Lebanon every bombed house was replaced by one built via the reconstruction fund; every destroyed school meant a chance to build a madrassa that would produce future Hezbollah fighters."[197]

A less aggressive form of coercion is the imposition of sanctions, and a number of countries have had the wrath of the international community visited on them using these means over the years. Amongst them have been Iraq in 1990, Haiti (1991), Libya (1992), Somalia (1992), Rwanda (1994), Afghanistan (1999) and Ethiopia and Eritrea (2000).[198]

After Saddam Hussein's invasion of Kuwait in August 1990, the United Nations imposed a blanket sanction on all trade with Iraq in an attempt to force him to withdraw. The sanctions failed to shift him, but UNICEF has estimated that the effect on the general population was so grim that half a million Iraqi children died from malnutrition. Iraq's occupation of Kuwait was only ended by the American-led invasion in January 1991.

The sanctions imposed on Haiti following the military coup in September 1991 also badly affected children. In what was already one of the poorest countries in the Western Hemisphere, in the three years that the sanctions were in place, the proportion of malnourished children under five increased from 27% to over 50%, and it has been estimated that thousands of children died as a result. All aspects of daily life were affected, including transportation, power supply and healthcare. Preventable diseases made a comeback. For example, as the number of measles vaccinations declined, the proportion of deaths from measles rose from 1% to 14% in a single year. However, the leaders of the coup, on whom the sanctions were supposed to exert pressure, were shielded from them by their wealth and power. Whilst they were able to buy what they needed on the black market, the people who really suffered were the already poverty-stricken ordinary citizens.[199]

A similar effect was felt when the UK Government imposed sanctions on Southern Rhodesia (now Zimbabwe) following its Unilateral Declaration of Independence in 1965. Whilst the white ruling class was barely affected, the poorest blacks were made even worse off.[200]

Sanctions have also tended to lead to increased levels of corruption, the strengthening of authoritarian rule and an increase in human rights violations in the affected country.[201] And even where they are aimed at specific people or a ruling elite, it has been found that there are still negative humanitarian outcomes in about half of the cases. Following the 1979 Tehran hostage crisis, when 52 Americans were held for 444 days by Iranian revolutionary students, the US imposed successive rounds of sanctions on Iran. Although the provision of medical and agricultural equipment and humanitarian assistance was still specifically allowed, most suppliers were so terrified of falling foul of the American authorities that they didn't dare take the risk. Even in 2014, a survey of over 100 executives from the London reinsurance market revealed that they would be very unlikely to underwrite a shipment of humanitarian aid to Iran, with one participant explaining that the due diligence required made it "just too difficult".[202]

Without going to the lengths of declaring war or imposing sanctions, communities can still show their displeasure at regimes of which they disapprove by imposing boycotts. Thus, for many years, music group U2 had a list of countries which they would not tour because of their poor human rights record. However, in 2010, U2 decided that this wasn't having the desired effect, and visited Turkey, previously high on their boycott list. And so, at a concert in Istanbul, 50,000 people showed their appreciation by joining in with Bono as he sang songs about peace, democracy and human rights. As Turkish novelist Elif Shafak has pointed out, as with other forms of sanction, cultural boycotts often have more effect on the people of a country rather than its government. Citizens of countries such as Turkey, Russia, Pakistan, Israel and others need to hear critical words, and U2's Istanbul concert was an opportunity for Bono to share his views publicly. A boycott, and the resulting absence of alternative external viewpoints, makes it easier for the oppressive forces in a country to spin their own line of rhetoric and build an inward-looking society. The musician Sting echoed these thoughts when he said of cultural boycotts that "they are counterproductive, where proscribed states are further robbed of the open commerce of ideas and art and as a result become even more closed, paranoid and insular." Radiohead's Thom Yorke agrees. When faced with criticism for playing concerts in Israel, he observed that, by refusing to play, "You're not bringing people together. You're not encouraging dialogue or a sense of understanding."[203] Elif Shafak welcomed the coming of U2 to Turkey, seeing their visit as an opportunity to strengthen those who were struggling against the Turkish

Government. And she said of boycotts in general, "We need to find more efficient methods of criticism. The impact of seeing Palestinian and Jewish artists collaborating is far greater than boycotts launched from a distance. It is better to go there, meet the people, give interviews to the media, spread the critical word."[204]

Undoubtedly the cultural boycott of South Africa, begun in the early 1960s, did much to highlight the evils of the apartheid regime, but adopting too broad-brush an approach may not be the most efficient way of achieving the desired result. Paul Simon brought the wrath of the artistic community on his head when he was seen to break the boycott by electing to record some of his ground-breaking 1986 *Graceland* album in South Africa. Although he was employing black South African musicians and paying them three times the going rate, he was widely condemned. But the huge success of that album meant that black South African music and the musicians who performed it were opened up to a far wider audience. The album became the most successful of Simon's stellar career, selling over 16 million copies, and enabled the South African artists he used, such as Ladysmith Black Mambazo and guitarist Ray Phiri, to develop their careers outside South Africa. In so doing, they were able to publicise much more effectively just what was happening in their country. As a result, Andrew Mueller of *Uncut* magazine felt able to write in 2012 that, "it would be absurd to suggest that Simon's introduction of South African music to the world prolonged it (Apartheid) and quite plausible to suggest that it did some small amount to hasten its undoing."

Wars, sanctions and boycotts. They all seem likely to give rise to unintended consequences. So might the solution lie in taking positive rather than negative action to right injustices and resolve conflicts?

From the day that the State of Israel was carved out of Palestine in 1948, the Palestinians have been in conflict with Israel, understandably feeling that they have been unjustly ejected from their own homeland in favour of the Jewish people. In the 1990s, new efforts were made to resolve this seemingly endless dispute, and it was felt that giving aid to both sides would help to oil negotiations and ease tensions. Aid was poured into the region, and in the 1990s more aid was given to the Palestinian Authority and the Israelis than to Rwanda, Bosnia or indeed to any other humanitarian crisis. The Palestinians received US$2.7 billion between 1993 and 1999, whilst the Israelis received an average of US$3 billion every year from the US. This money was given to support the 1993 and 1995 Oslo Accords, which were agreements that had been initiated by the Norwegian Government and signed by the multiparty representatives of the Palestinians, the Palestinian Liberation Organisation (PLO) and the Israeli Government, with the hope that they would bring a "just, lasting and comprehensive peace settlement" to Gaza and the West Bank. The aid was intended to help prepare the way for Palestinian statehood and was channelled through PLO leader Yasser Arafat so that, by giving him a personal stake, he would be encouraged to continue with the discussions when they got bogged down.

Aid from the international community funded the employment of 120,000 Palestinians, but they actually received their wages from the PLO, and so looked to them for their livelihood. Taking their dependents into account, this meant that almost half of the residents of the West Bank and Gaza were reliant on the PLO, at a time when other employment was extremely hard to come by. However, the PLO tended to give most of these jobs to members of Yasser Arafat's own party, Fatah, and it was groups aligned to Fatah who received the bulk of the financial assistance, whereas others, including those connected with the Islamic opposition, were cut off by Arafat. As the terms of the Peace Accords prevented the Palestinians from developing economically, a large minority in Palestine either seeing no improvement or actually being worse off despite the aid. Indeed, a poll taken in 2000 indicated that 50% of Gazans and 43% of West Bankers felt that their standard of living had fallen since the beginning of the Oslo process.[205] Consequently, as the 1990s drew to a close, there were large numbers of disaffected young men who, unable to earn a living and ostracised by the PLO, were drawn towards violent groups such as Hamas and Islamic Jihad.

And so it was that, after 7 long years of intense effort and huge amounts of aid, in September 2000 the Palestinians resumed their intifada against Israel, resulting in not only the metaphorical death of the peace process but also the actual deaths of about 1,000 Israelis and 3,200 Palestinians over the following five years.[206]

Rather than pouring oil on troubled water, the aid that had flooded into the region had served to alienate a considerable portion of the Palestinians, alienation that eventually led to the resumption of full-blown hostilities with the Israelis.

Elsewhere in the world, just as the Oslo Accords were coming into effect, the troubles in the Middle East were being dwarfed by the most appalling genocide in Africa. Tucked underneath the south-west corner of Uganda and to the west of Tanzania, Rwanda is a country about the same size as the state of Massachusetts or one and a quarter Waleses. For many years tension had been growing in the country between the two main ethnic groups, the Hutus, who comprised about 85% of the population, and the Tutsis, who made up most of the rest. Division of Rwandans into their ethnic groups had been facilitated by the introduction, in 1933, of compulsory identity cards, specifying the holder's ethnic background. For many years the Tutsis had held political control of the country, but in a revolt by the Hutus in 1959, the Tutsi regime was overthrown and a campaign of racist persecution against the Tutsis began. By 1990 over 600,000 Tutsis had been forced to take refuge abroad, mainly in Uganda and other nearby countries.

The Rwandan economy was in a dreadful state, due largely to the collapse in coffee prices in the late 1980s and a series of droughts. As coffee was one of the main Rwandan exports, the country's foreign earnings halved between 1987 and 1991. At the same time, some of the Tutsi refugees who had been forced north to Uganda formed the Rwandan Patriotic Front, an organisation dedicated to enabling the Tutsi exiles to return to their homeland, and in 1990 they began conducting a guerrilla war in the northern part of Rwanda.

With Hutu extremists and some of the press whipping up a violent anti-Tutsi atmosphere, in April 1994 the powder-keg was lit by the assassination of the Rwandan President Habyarimana, a moderate Hutu, when the plane on which he was travelling (together with the new President of neighbouring Burundi) was shot down by two missiles as it came in to land at Rwanda's Kigali Airport.

This was immediately followed by the murder of the Prime Minister and other moderate Hutu leaders, and the Hutu population began a massacre of the hated Tutsis in an attempt to completely wipe them out. They were all too horribly successful. About three-quarters of the Tutsis, at least 800,000 men, women and children, were murdered in a few weeks, often in the most brutal ways, together with anyone else who tried to stand in the way of the rampaging mobs.

Tragically, international aid had helped to bring about this ghastly state of affairs. Faced with Rwanda's economic problems in the early 1990s, Western aid agencies attempted to help, but insisted that the country move towards democratisation and improved respect for human rights and the rule of law. A multiparty political system was introduced, which enabled the formation of racist Hutu political parties, who were violently opposed to what they saw as the appeasement of the Tutsis. However, the international community felt that Rwanda was failing to comply with their requirements, and so the US withdrew all but humanitarian aid, and the World Bank and EU also threatened to withhold promised monies. President Habyarimana was forced to compromise and in August 1993 entered into a series of agreements called the Arusha Accords, which were designed to end the guerrilla war by integrating the Rwandan Patriotic Front into the country's armed forces and giving them a place in the Government.[207] With conditions still not improving, aid was cut back again at the beginning of 1994, forcing President Habyarimana to give the RPF roles in the running of the country and the military. The extremist Hutu parties were violently opposed to this, and began to plan and prepare for the massacre of Tutsis in revenge.

With the assassination of the president in April 1994, his opponents, who had been both nurtured and threatened by the conditions imposed by the Accords, unleashed their genocidal massacre of the Tutsis and anyone else who opposed them.

Quite what the rest of the world could have done to prevent the Rwandan massacres is debatable, but it does seem that the well-meaning conditions attached to the Accords were instrumental in facilitating the actions that took place in those dreadful few weeks in 1994.

Aid failed to help resolve the political issues in the Middle East and Rwanda, but the potential for aid-giving to backfire was something that the IMF, World Bank and US Treasury were in fact well aware of. Inspired by the success of East Asian economies such as South Korea and Malaysia, they wanted to ensure that aid given to Latin America and sub-Saharan African countries was accompanied by economic reform, thereby enabling the recipient to achieve economic growth and bring themselves out of poverty. As Harvard economist Professor Dani Rodrik has written, "Observing the endless list of policy follies to which poor nations had succumbed, any well-trained and well-intentioned economist could feel justified in uttering the obvious truths of the profession: get your macro balances in order, take the state out of business, give markets free rein."[208] And so, in 1990 the IMF, World Bank and US Treasury adopted 10 rules which were to govern the giving of aid to economically struggling countries. This was the "Washington Consensus", so-called because the three organisations were all based in Washington DC.

By now, you can probably see where this is going. When Kenya, as directed by the IMF, reduced the barriers to trade on cotton and imported clothing, the result was a flood of cheap imports and second-hand clothing into the country. Although the US was very quick to demand that markets elsewhere should be free, it was happy at the same time to subsidise its own cotton producers, thereby enabling them to export to Kenya and elsewhere at 40% below the cost of production. Kenya's own cotton production found itself unable to compete and was devastated. By the end of the 1990s, the value of Kenya's cotton production had fallen to one-twentieth of the 1980s output.[209] As trade restrictions on textiles were phased out in other parts of Africa, more than 250,000 jobs were lost across the continent as a result.[210]

And these problems were not just confined to textiles. In 2003 the Ghanaian parliament attempted to protect Ghanaian farmers by increasing import tariffs on poultry. Even though this was allowed by the World Trade Organization's rules, the IMF objected on behalf of the aid-giving nations and Ghana was forced to withdraw the increased tariff. The result was that subsidised European imports were dumped on the Ghanaian market, and by 2011 imports of poultry into Ghana had increased from under 14,000 metric tons in 2000 to more than 155,000 in 2011, once again causing havoc to the local economy, achieving the opposite of the aim of the aid donors.[211, 212] And, across sub-Saharan Africa as a whole, under the regime of the supposedly helpful Washington Consensus, Gross Domestic Product per head actually shrank by an average 0.1% per year between 1990 and 2001.[213]

As Economics Nobel Laureate Joseph Stiglitz observed in 2004, when it comes to the best strategies to help poor countries, "There is no consensus, except that the Washington Consensus did not provide the answer."[214]

This is not the only issue with aid. The officials receiving it are not always completely trustworthy, and Professor Jeffrey Winters, of Northwestern University, argued before a US Senate committee in 2004 that about US$100 billion (about £77 billion) of World Bank funds, intended for development, had been corruptly misused. As Zambian economist Dambisa Moyo has concluded, "Evidence overwhelmingly demonstrates that aid to Africa has made the poor poorer, and the growth slower."[215]

Of course, this is not to deny for one moment the value of aid which is properly targeted and which works for the benefit of the recipient. Fresh drinking water, food, disease eradication, supply of power and education have all been provided by various benefactors, including aid agencies and charities, some massive, some tiny, and have helped many communities in Africa. One of the characteristics of helpful aid is that it tends to go directly to those in need, bypassing the local government, and thereby reducing the problems of inefficient distribution and any tendency for the government to siphon it off or use the aid for its own political advantage.

However (and doesn't it seem as though there is always a "however"?), even this type of targeted giving can still backfire. Dambisa Moyo posits the example of a well-meaning Western organisation that donated 100,000 mosquito nets to a part of Africa where malaria is endemic. This looks like a good thing, but it doesn't take into account the plight of the existing mosquito net maker, who may be employing 10 people, each of whom supports more than 15 relatives. With the mosquito net market flooded, he goes out of business, and 150 people are left worse off. And the consequences don't end there, because when the free nets become broken and need replacing, there is no local maker to supply them, and so further help from abroad will be sought.[216] Student Christina Field discovered a real-life example when she travelled to Malawi to see how much help people were getting from gifts of second-hand clothes which had been sent by Western charities. She found that, whilst the recipients themselves were very grateful, importing garments free of charge was having a terrible effect on the local textile industry.[217]

Chapter 5

Scientific progress – that's a good thing, right?

As Victor Frankenstein has illustrated, the wrong sort of scientific progress can have its downsides.

Indeed, science has been backfiring pretty much since its earliest days. Back in the 9th century CE, Chinese alchemists were very keen to discover the key to immortality, and in their quest were constantly experimenting with combinations of substances. One experimental mixture combined saltpetre, sulphur and charcoal, resulting in a powder which, when its explosive properties were fully appreciated, came to be known as gunpowder. The authorities quickly latched on to its destructive potential and established factories which produced poetically-named weapons such as the "eight-sided, magical, awe-inspiring wind and fire cannon" and the "nine arrows, heart penetrating, magically poisonous fire-thunderer". Such was their enthusiasm for this new weaponry that by 1160, the Imperial armaments office was producing 3.2 million such weapons a year. In their search for immortality, the alchemists had inadvertently produced a substance that would instead cut short untold lives.

Even just storing gunpowder can be lethal, as the mixture is unstable and liable to explode with the slightest provocation. In the 16th and 17th centuries, an arms race resulted in the demand for gunpowder rising inexorably, with London at the centre of the trade. However, despite taking precautions, there were constant accidental explosions. For example, in April 1583 an explosion in Fetter Lane destroyed a number of houses and the "monstrous and huge blast of the gunpowder" shattered the windows in two churches: St Andrews, 150 yards away in one direction, and the chapel of Lincoln's Inn, a quarter of a mile the other way. In

1650, one Robert Porter left 20 barrels of gunpowder in his shop in Tower Street, ready to be collected the next day. However, the gunpowder exploded, destroying 15 houses and damaging over 100 others, killing 67 people in the process. And London wasn't the only city to have problems with gunpowder storage. In the 16th century alone there were major explosions in Dublin, Venice, Delft, Basel, Luxembourg and Leiden.[218]

Producing gunpowder is even more dangerous. In May 1838, following an explosion at a Cornish gunpowder mill, one newspaper reported that:

> *A most dreadful explosion occurred at the Kennall Gunpowder Mills, near Penryn, on Tuesday morning, the 10th instant. Five mills blew up in succession, and part of a roof was found a mile from the premises.*

Mercifully, only one man was killed in the incident.[219]

Deadlier explosives have since been developed, but often with the same dangers, and in 1864 an explosion at a factory manufacturing nitroglycerine in Sweden killed 6 people. One of these was a man named Emil Nobel. His elder brother Alfred, determined to prevent this type of accident recurring, experimented with various forms of the explosive, and by 1867 had come up with the formula for dynamite, which had enormous destructive force but was much less prone to explode at the wrong time. Alfred's avowed hope was that not only would lives be saved in its manufacture, but that, because its use would be so deadly, men would hold back from conducting war and, in Alfred's words, "abide by golden peace". In a conversation with his secretary in 1876, he said that he had wanted to produce "a substance or machine of such frightful efficacy for wholesale devastation that war should thereby become altogether impossible"[220] and he later expressed the view that, "On the day when two army corps will be able to annihilate each other in one second, all civilised nations will recoil from war in horror and disband their forces."[221] However, as his biographer Herta E. Pauli wryly observed, "What then if an uncivilised one appears?", going on to make the point that, "the theory, of increasing the horror of war to deter men from waging it, is one of the most colossal fallacies in the history of human thought."[222]

Just a few years earlier, Richard Gatling had also been working with the most humanitarian of intentions. He had noticed that, in the American Civil War, the greatest cause of death amongst soldiers was not from actually fighting, but from illnesses that they picked up in camp. He felt that the solution was a machine that could reduce the number of soldiers required to fight a war. He therefore set about inventing a gun that "could by its rapidity of fire, enable one man to do as much battle duty as a hundred, that it would, to a large extent supersede the necessity of large armies, and consequently, exposure to battle and disease would be greatly diminished." In 1862 he patented the Gatling Gun, a machine gun mounted on wheels and capable of firing upwards of 150 rounds a minute, and his gun went on to be used in warfare with deadly effect for many years. However, as Gatling somehow seemed not to have twigged, possession of the gun gave a huge advantage to any army that had it against an opposition that did not. The gun hugely benefited European colonial empires, who used it to mow down large numbers of indigenous fighters who were armed only with tribal weapons.

Orville Wright had similar high hopes for the aeroplane. He felt that, by enabling aerial reconnaissance, which could provide much more accurate information about the position of the enemy, warfare would become much more efficient, and so the aeroplane would, in his words, "put an end to war." Once again, that fond hope was smashed to pieces, and as the citizens of Coventry, Dresden, Hiroshima, Nagasaki and all too many other places around the world could bitterly attest, reconnaissance was not the only use that planes could be put to.

Other inventions have backfired in a more subtle but nonetheless dramatic way. Early refrigerators used ammonia as a coolant although it is highly toxic. In his search for a safer alternative, inventor Thomas Midgley discovered something called CFC (chlorofluorocarbon), Freon, which from the 1960s replaced ammonia as a supposedly clean refrigerant. However, by the late 1980s it had become clear that this supposedly safe alternative was playing havoc with the Earth's protective ozone layer, with potentially devastating consequences for the whole planet. Concerted worldwide action resulted in CFCs being banned in 1995. They were replaced in many instances by HFCs (hydrofluorocarbons), which are much the same chemical, but without the ozone-damaging chlorine. However, in a perhaps all too familiar turn of events, it was then discovered that HFCs are also terrible for the environment, being greenhouse gases thousands of times more powerful than carbon dioxide. In 2016 agreement was reached to phase out HFCs with a range of less harmful alternatives.

In the battles between Humankind and Nature, there often seems to be an underlying assumption that if we make enough effort, Nature will bend to our will. However, Nature is a formidable opponent and has many ways of biting back. Just after Christmas 2013, many people in the UK became only too aware of their powerlessness in the face of Nature's might. As storms battered the country, more rain fell in one month than in any other over the previous 100 years. The Somerset Levels, 170,000 acres (265 square miles) of flat landscape in the south-west of England, were particularly badly hit. Covered by the sea in ancient times, much of the area lies less than 12 feet (4 metres) above sea level, and since the Roman era it has been artificially drained to provide farmland. A number of rivers run through the area but, unable to cope with the huge amount of rainwater streaming off the surrounding Quantock and Mendip Hills, they burst their banks, flooding about 17,000 acres (26 square miles) of farmland. Matters progressively worsened, and within a month, 600 houses had been flooded and transport links broken. Whole villages were cut off, and in mid-February the town of Bridgwater was partly flooded. Local people demanded that something be done, and the loudest voices called for the rivers to be dredged so that the water could run away more quickly. The then Prime Minister, David Cameron, responded to these calls by promising that once the waters had dropped sufficiently, dredging would take place, and indeed, by the end of March, dredging of the rivers Parrett and Tone began, with the avowed intention of increasing their capacity by up to 40%. Nature had done its worst, but in the end, Humankind had prevailed.

Or so one might have thought. However, as is so often the case, an obvious solution is not necessarily the right one. David Cameron seemed to be unaware of the concerns of the UK Environment Agency, which had pointed out in a presentation called "To Dredge Or Not To Dredge?" that the capacity of a river is tiny in comparison to its catchment area. If a river suddenly has to cope with, say, three times its usual flow of water, then increasing the flow by 40% by dredging the river will do little to reduce the amount of flooding. Worse still, by moving the water on more quickly, the dredging makes things worse for towns downstream. Where there are towns, there will be bridges, and when the increased flow reaches them, the water, now travelling faster and carrying all sorts of detritus, will hit these artificial pinch-points and the river will be forced to rise. As it does so, it threatens the safety of the bridges and the likelihood of the town flooding, thereby causing far more economic damage and danger to life than that caused by any flooding of the fields upstream.

It is perhaps not sufficiently appreciated that rivers are the natural way by which excess rainfall makes its way from the hills to the sea. In attempting to tinker with them, usually by straightening out inconvenient kinks or otherwise encouraging the water to flow more quickly, planners can all too easily create problems elsewhere. The answer may therefore be to undo some of the earlier tinkering. Former director of Friends of the Earth, Tony Juniper, has suggested that it is not only meddling with the rivers that causes the problems, but that mismanagement of the upland areas over the generations has contributed to these floods. Writing in *The Guardian* newspaper, he suggested that, "The degradation of peat soils by burning, drainage and the cutting of peat for fuel means that the many areas of blanket bog that clothe Britain's hills and mountains can no longer serve their function as giant sponges that collect and hold rain."[223] It would be wise to improve these areas not only by not removing the peat, but by allowing the hills to reforest (rather than being grazed by sheep) so that the tree roots could help to absorb rainwater at source and prevent it from entering the river system in the first place.

In December 2015, just two years after the Somerset flooding, it was the north of England that was hit by record levels of rainfall, and towns across Cumbria and Yorkshire suffered dreadfully from flooding. Whalley in East Lancashire was completely swamped when the River Calder burst its banks, and parts of the cities of York and Leeds had to be evacuated. There were extensive blackouts after flood defences were breached at a number of electricity substations, a sinkhole opened on the M62 motorway in Greater Manchester and the 18th-century bridge across the river Wharfe at Tadcaster was swept away. And all this was despite government funded flood defence schemes that had been put in place over the previous 20 years in order to prevent these consequences.

However, one town did manage to stay dry, which was interesting, as the Government had refused its application for flood defences. Pickering in North Yorkshire lies at the bottom of a steep gorge which drains much of the North York Moors, and the town had been flooded 4 times between 1999 and 2007, with the damage on the last occasion having cost £7 million (about US$9 million) to repair. The Environment Agency considered spending £20 million (about US$26 million) on building a concrete wall through the middle of the town to safeguard it from future floods, but as well as looking very ugly, the scheme had failed the cost-benefit test imposed by the Treasury and so was abandoned. After this succession of floods, and turned down by the Government, the local people were, in the words of Mike Potter, chairman of the Pickering and District Civic Society, "spitting feathers", and they decided to seek a solution themselves. A local environmentalist pointed out that the moors surrounding the town had traditionally retained rainwater for a much longer period, and so, working with academics from various universities, it was decided to attempt to return to the old ways. Following their research, local bodies, working with the Environment Agency, Forestry Commission and Department of Environment, Food and Rural Affairs, put their plan into action. They built 167 "leaky" dams of logs and branches in the surrounding becks, so that normal flows could pass through, but torrents would be held back. They added 187 other obstructions made of bales of heather in smaller gullies and planted 40,000 trees. Then, inspired by the example of the medieval monks at nearby Byland Abbey, they built a type of embankment called a "bund", which could hold back up to 120,000 cubic metres of floodwater, for gradual release through a culvert. This "Slowing The Flow" scheme was completed in September 2015, just three months before the storms hit. The measures that had been put in place reduced the peak flow of the river through Pickering by 20%, enough to ensure that the town didn't flood and its inhabitants were able to get on with life as normal. And the cost of these defences? A mere £2 million (about US$2.6 million), a tenth of the cost of the proposed wall and about a quarter of the cost of clearing up after the floods of 2007. And as well as the financial benefit, the people of the town had avoided the emotional trauma that being flooded brings.[224] Whilst the flood defences introduced across the rest of the region had largely failed, the unintended consequence of refusing Pickering the "obvious" solution of a £20 million (about US$26 million) wall meant that the town turned to a scheme borne of desperation – but a scheme which turned out to be successful as well as cheaper.

Similar schemes have worked successfully in Glasgow and Somerset, whilst the construction of a nature reserve at Potteric Carr in Yorkshire protected the south of Doncaster in 2007. Whilst the north of the city was flooded, the south was kept dry.[225] Rather than adopting the seemingly obvious course of action, which may actually make things worse, this is just one situation where a more nuanced approach is the way to go. Instead of looking for artificial solutions, just properly maintaining the countryside can have a dramatic effect. Peat bogs, for example, can comprise 90% water, so leaving peat in the ground rather than digging it up for use in garden compost or to burn in power stations stops a lot of water running straight into the nearest river. Other steps such as replanting trees on hillsides and not burning heather on grouse moors also help to hold water back from the local river system.

The National Trust is one organisation that appears to have taken on board the wisdom of this strategy. In August 2016, it purchased 300-acre Thorneythwaite Farm in the Lake District, with the avowed intention of replacing the sheep-farming monoculture so that, when combined with other local land already under their control:

> ... we can take a "big picture" view of how we manage the wider landscape, and it allows us to focus on delivering healthy soil, natural water management, thriving natural habitats and continued public access. We will also explore how we may be able to use the farm to slow the flow of the Upper River Derwent, thereby contributing

to the prevention of flooding downstream in communities such as Keswick and Cockermouth.[226]

As scientific knowledge continues to expand, ethical questions regarding its development and use become ever more important. To take one current example, the possibility of not only reading DNA but actually writing it is leading some in the scientific community to explore how we might bring about the so-called "de-extinction" of animals, resurrecting creatures that have died out, even though the *Jurassic Park* films have illustrated some of the potential dangers in doing so. But whilst it appears that dinosaurs are actually just too far gone to bring back, close copies of other more recent extinctions for which viable DNA still exists, such as mammoths, the American passenger pigeon (of which more later) or the Tasmanian tiger, could quite possibly be created. However, thoughtlessly bringing something into a new habitat is wrought with potential problems.

Victorian England provides us with all too many examples. With untold wealth being acquired by those taking advantage of the Industrial Revolution and the spread of the British Empire, there was huge pressure to give one's magnificent estate a unique twist. One of the ways of doing this was to have plants in the garden that couldn't be seen elsewhere. Plant hunters such as Joseph Hooker and John Veitch went on expeditions around the globe with the aim of collecting and bringing back the most exotic plants, with gardeners competing to show off the latest and most dramatic. Hooker brought back many rhododendrons from the Himalayas, whilst Veitch was one of the first plant hunters to visit Japan. Another Japanese collector was Philipp von Siebold, who in 1850 sent a number of plants to the Royal Botanical Gardens at Kew in London. Amongst the imports was one that he called Polygonum sieboldii, but which came to be known as Japanese knotweed. It is a decorative plant which grows to about 6 feet high and makes a real statement in a garden, and it quickly became popular with commercial nurseries around the country. However, what was not appreciated at the time was exactly how much of a statement it would make, not only in British gardens but also along railway embankments, where it was grown for its stabilising properties. Uninhibited in its welcoming new habitat, its roots spread with enormous vigour and have proven capable of growing through pretty much anything, even house foundations and road surfaces. Once established, it is almost impossible (and extremely costly) to get rid of. Such a pest has it become that, if it is growing nearby, it can reduce a house's value or make it difficult to sell at all. The cost of controlling it, combined with its effect on property prices, is currently around £166 million (about US$216 million) a year. However, it has been calculated that it would cost about £1.5 billion (about US$2 billion) to actually eradicate it, which has led the UK's Department for Environment, Food and Rural Affairs to say that it has no plans to attempt such a course of action. Disastrous though its introduction has been, it looks as though we are stuck with it.

Himalayan balsam (Impatiens glandulifera) is another plant that was introduced to the UK at about the same time, and it too has adapted only too well to conditions in Britain. Growing up to 10 feet high, and ideally suited to shady spots where other plants struggle, it has colonised many river banks, where it crowds out the native species and where its distinctive purple flowers have become a familiar sight.

Whilst Japanese knotweed and Himalayan balsam were being imported into Britain, British colonists who had moved to south-eastern Australia discovered a strange yearning for the blackberry, and so had some brambles brought from home. As anyone who has brambles in their garden will be unsurprised to learn, it wasn't long before the plant spread out of control, which it has continued to do to this day. As if its ability to form dense thickets of impenetrably spiky undergrowth wasn't enough, it also provides protection for other interlopers such as pigs and rabbits. Gorse, another early 19th-century introduction to Australia, has also become a major problem, especially in Tasmania and parts of Victoria. The Australian Government has estimated that imported weeds now account for about 15% of Australia's total plants and cost farmers A$1.5 billion (over £800 million, or US$1 billion) a year in weed control and a further A$2.5 billion (almost £1.4 billion, or over US$1.8 billion) a year in lost agricultural production.[227] So seriously does the Government now take this problem that, in a bid to prevent new incursions, any visitors to Australia will have their belongings examined extremely thoroughly before they are allowed into the country.

Colonists arriving in America did much the same thing, importing blackberry and gorse along with a variety of other plants from home. As in Australia, many promptly went native. Even such an apparent innocent as purple loosestrife, introduced from Europe as an ornamental plant in the early 19th century, has been spreading across America at a rate of about 320,000 acres (500 square miles) per year. It loves wetlands, where it is able to outcompete native plants, and it threatens wildlife such as the bog turtle and a number of duck species by reducing their food supply. Loosestrife alone costs the US economy about US$45 million (about £35 million) per year. Parts of California have their particular horror story in the yellow starthistle. Probably introduced in contaminated animal feed during the mid-19th-century Gold Rush, it is a real thug of a plant, often growing over 4-feet high in dense stands. It outcompetes neighbouring plants by sucking the available moisture and nutrients from the soil with a taproot that can burrow up to 8-feet down, whilst a square metre (10 square feet) clump can produce up to 29,000 seeds, of which 95%, carried far and wide by the wind, will germinate.[228] As a result, over 30,000 square miles (over 19 million acres, or about the size of the Czech Republic) of once-grazed Californian grassland has been completely ruined.[229] It has been estimated that weeds introduced to America have now colonised an area equal to the entire state of California and cost the economy an enormous US$30 billion (about £23 billion) per year.[230]

And that is just the plants. Rabbits, pigs, cats and dogs have all gone feral after being brought into America and Australia, whilst accidental imports such as black and brown rats also have an enormous impact. The rats alone cause damage of over US$19 billion (about £15 billion) per year to grain and other property in America, whilst aquatic creatures such as quagga and zebra mussels which, introduced accidentally to the Great Lakes in ships' ballast, thrive so successfully that densities of up to 700,000 mussels per square metre (10 square feet) have been found. As well as killing off indigenous molluscs, they can clog water intake pipes, filters and electric generating plants at an estimated cost of US$1 billion (about £770 million) per year. In 2005 it was estimated that the total annual cost to the US economy of all invasive species was a staggering US$120 billion (about £92 million).[231]

But, as with plants, the traffic has not been entirely one way. I grew up in the south-east of England and clearly remember as a child seeing beautiful red squirrels skipping through the branches in local woods. However, my children see only the grey squirrel which, in most of England, has now usurped the red. Introduced from America in the 1870s as an exotic attraction for country estates, it has outcompeted the red so successfully that it is estimated there are now more than 100 grey squirrels for every red.[232]

Sadly, virtually every country seems to be able to tell a similar tale. In Germany, just one man was responsible for an ecological disaster. That man was Herman Goering, who in 1934 had what one might have thought was a fairly harmless job as the Third Reich's chief forester. However, in that year he took it upon himself to introduce a pair of American raccoons into a German wood, as he felt that it would be nice for hunters to have the opportunity to shoot them. However, the raccoons evaded the hunters and prospered, in which they were helped by the outbreak of the Second World War, when the hunters took their guns elsewhere. Raccoons aren't content to confine themselves to woods, but enjoy living under houses, as these provide both a safe refuge and a ready source of food from rubbish bins. However, as winter comes on and the weather gets colder, the raccoons have a tendency to break into the houses in search of food and warmth. Thus it was that one German family returned from holiday to discover that a raccoon had climbed down their chimney and had eaten all the food in their cupboards, whilst in 2002 a family of raccoons broke into the house of Ingrid and Dieter Hoffmann in the city of Kassel, in central Germany, taking up residence in the chimney and resisting all attempts to smoke them out. They wrecked the roof before they were finally removed, and the Hoffmanns were forced to install electrified gutters and other deterrents to stop them returning. German pest controllers now estimate that there are at least a million raccoons at large in the country and predict that they will never be eradicated. They now range from the Baltic Sea to the Alps and have been spotted as far east as Chechnya, and all because of the thoughtless act of one man.[233, 234]

Many and varied attempts have been made to deal with invasive species, some with reasonable success. Thus, the tsetse fly, accidentally introduced to the island of Principe in the Gulf of Guinea in 1825, where it caused devastating sleeping sickness, was eradicated between 1911 and 1914 by a plucky team of three hundred people who walked about the island wearing black cloths coated with birdlime.[235] In 1954, scientists carried out a successful experiment to rid the island of Curaçao of the potentially lethal screw-worm fly. Despite facing some mockery at the time, they flooded the island with huge numbers of sterilised male screw-worm flies. The females (who mate only once) failed to reproduce, and within 6 months the problem was solved.[236]

However, there have been people who, in attempting to get rid of a pest, have not heeded the warning contained in a familiar song from my youth. *I Know an Old Lady*, sung by Burl Ives, relates the tale of an old lady who had rather annoyingly swallowed a fly. It is in fact a classic saga of unintended consequences, as the old lady attempts to get rid of the fly by swallowing a spider. The spider then needs to be caught, as do each of the succeeding solutions, so that she sequentially swallows a bird, a cat, a dog and a cow, until finally, she swallows a horse. Clearly, this was not going to end happily, and indeed the outcome was fatal for the old lady. Had she only thought a little more about the probable consequences before embarking on this course of action, her life would have been longer (although the song very much shorter).

Unfortunately, there are all too many cases where her example has been followed in real life. In 1872, Jamaica was having a terrible time with rats in its sugar cane plantations. So some Indian mongooses were introduced to the island in order to kill the rats. The mongooses managed to control the brown rat, but not the black, and they didn't stop at rats, but also preyed on ground-nesting birds, amphibians and reptiles,[237] and they now threaten the nests of the Hawksbill and Green Sea Turtles. In 1883, Hawaii did exactly the same thing, with inevitably much the same effect on its local wildlife.

In 1777, rabbits were introduced to New Zealand in order to provide food and hunting. However, by the 1880s they were threatening the habitat of the nation's wildlife, overrunning sheep stations and posing a serious threat to the economy. And so, to catch them, New Zealand imported ferrets, followed by boatloads of stoats and weasels brought from the UK. Tragically and inevitably, these predators ruthlessly feasted on New Zealand's defenceless native birds and animals.

Some 50 years later, sugar cane farmers in Queensland also found that they were having problems, but this time from the depredations of the cane beetle. However, they ignored any lessons that history might have taught them, and the Australian Bureau of Sugar Experimental Stations decided to release 101 Hawaiian cane toads in order to catch the cane beetle. But the cane toad is not choosy about its food, and promptly turned to eating pretty much whatever it could catch, including small snakes, mice, lizards and even bees. It is also extremely fecund, with females laying up to 30,000 eggs each year, and long-lived, with a possible lifespan of 15 years. As if that weren't enough, the toads are poisonous and can prove fatal to would-be predators. As a consequence, the cane toad has spread so successfully that hundreds of millions of them now cover an area of 100,000 square miles (64 million acres, or one New Zealand) of Australia, and they continue their march westward at an estimated 25–40 miles (40–64 km) per year. Enormous effort is being expended in attempting to eradicate them, or at least limit their spread, but this is extremely costly and, to be frank, largely ineffective. In 2010 the Australian Government admitted that it is unlikely that there will ever be a way to control the cane toad.[238]

But perhaps the place that best exemplifies the folly of the Old Lady is Macquarie Island, a tiny pencil-shaped strip of land, 21 miles (34 km) long and 3 (5 km) wide, that lies about halfway between New Zealand and Antarctica. With one of the greatest concentrations of breeding seabirds anywhere in the world, including large numbers of penguins, it was first visited by Europeans in 1810, who promptly set about killing the island's seals and penguins for their fur and blubber. These visits allowed rats and mice to escape from ships on to the island and, having no natural predators, the rodents were able to multiply freely. They ravaged the sailors' food stores, and so, in about 1820, cats were introduced to control them. An uneasy balance ensued for about fifty years, at which time rabbits were brought to the island to provide an additional food source. Inevitably, some escaped, multiplying to such an extent that they devastated the island's vegetation. This resulted in soil erosion, some of which was so severe that whole cliffs collapsed. So in 1978, myxomatosis was introduced in order to kill off the rabbits, and it was so brutally successful that their numbers fell from 130,000 to 20,000 within 10 years. However, in the meantime, the feral population of cats had come to rely on the rabbits for food, and so, as the rabbits became scarcer, the cats turned instead to catching the native birds, to such an extent that, by the mid-1980s, the island's seabird population was being seriously affected. War was declared on the cats, and by 2001 they had been successfully eradicated. It probably won't come as a surprise to learn that this was still not the end of the saga. With the cats gone, the few hardy rabbits that were immune to myxomatosis began to multiply, and soon the plants and soil were suffering again. Things came to a head in 2006 when rabbit depredation caused a landslip that destroyed an important penguin colony. After almost 200 years of unintended consequences, it wasn't until 2009 that a report recommended that, rather than adopting a piecemeal, *I Know an Old Lady* approach, it would be necessary to deal comprehensively with the invaders.[239] Consequently A$24 million (just under £12 million or US$16 million) was budgeted to pay for a programme of simultaneous eradication of rabbits, rats and mice from the island. The process was complicated, involving a combination of poison bait dropped by helicopter and the introduction of calicivirus to kill off the rabbits, whilst hunters on the ground worked with specially trained dogs to flush out any remaining rabbits and rodents. Mercifully, they managed to ensure that no dogs escaped. By the end of 2011, the island was completely pest free and its wildlife was beginning to recover.[240]

So, should we be so unfortunate as to swallow a metaphorical fly, we might do well to consider putting up with a little bit of metaphorical coughing, rather than thoughtlessly starting on a course of action which could spiral out of control. If steps are to be taken, they need to be well-thought out. But of course, as the Australians and others have now realised, the best plan of all is to have your metaphorical flypaper in place from the beginning, so that the metaphorical flies are not swallowed in the first place.

Whilst extermination might appear to be a straightforward (if brutal) solution to this type of problem, the actual process needs to be carefully considered lest it leads to something called the "Cobra Effect", so named after an episode reputed to have occurred in colonial India.* Apparently, the Government in Delhi became concerned about the danger posed by the large number of venomous cobras in the city. They therefore offered a reward for each dead cobra brought in. This was a great success, and huge numbers of dead cobras were soon piling up. However, there didn't seem to be any reduction in the number of cobras roaming the city, and upon investigation, the authorities discovered that, giving full vent to their entrepreneurial spirit, people had been setting up farms to breed cobras as this was very much easier than capturing them in the wild. Naturally, the Government promptly scrapped the bounty. This, however, left the farmers with a lot of valueless snakes, and so they just released them into the wild, thereby making the situation far worse than it had been before the Government acted. A very similar sequence of events happened in French Colonial Vietnam, although this time it was rats that were farmed in order to collect the bounty.[241]

A modern-day twist was discovered by Stephen Dubner and Steven Levitt, and related in one of their "Freakonomics" podcasts. When Spanish explorers made their initial forays to America, they very sensibly brought food with them, which included live pigs. As always seems to be the case, some escaped into the wild, and they took very happily to life in America, where there are now millions of them roaming free in the forests. As anyone who has seen pigs in action will know, they can be extremely destructive, digging up pretty well anything in their search for roots to eat.

About a thousand wild pigs made a particular nuisance of themselves at one US Army base in south-western Georgia. Fort Benning covers about 287 square miles (180,000 acres), almost half the size of Surrey, but only 120,000 people live on the base, which is surrounded by a lot of beautiful open countryside. In 2007 the US military, fed up with the damage caused by the pigs, offered a US$40 (about £30) bounty for each pig killed, to be evidenced by production of a pig's tail. You can probably see where this is going. Indeed, within a year of the programme's introduction, the bounty had been paid out on over a thousand pigs. Job done, one might think. However, the US military is nothing if not thorough, and so conducted a further survey just to make sure that all of the pigs were gone. However, it transpired that there were in fact now *more* pigs on the base than there had been at the start of the scheme. After some research, a number of issues with the programme were discovered. Quite a few pigs' tails had just been bought from butchers and other sources, meaning that in fact the number of pigs actually killed was nowhere near a thousand. To make things worse, hunters had been obtaining leftover food from local cafeterias to use as pig-bait. This included butter, meat, bread-rolls and other highly nutritious food, all of which was very attractive to pigs. The pigs accordingly scoffed the pig-bait, and the hunters duly shot as many of them as they could. However, once bullets started flying, the unshot pigs very sensibly ran away. Having enjoyed their free meal, and being intelligent animals, they learned to be a bit more cautious next time. So when they heard a hunter arriving in a car, they took cover and became much harder to shoot. And the pigs that got away grew fitter and healthier on their new high-protein diet, and consequently produced a lot more little pigs. As podcast producer Katherine Wells observed, "All the hunters had really been doing was playing a giant, unwinnable game of Whackamole."[242]

Rather than assume that people will respond to an incentive

scheme as we want, it would seem wise for those devising such a scheme to try to put themselves in the shoes of those receiving the incentives, and try to imagine how the system could possibly be gamed before going ahead with it.

We have seen how introduced species can wreak havoc on native wildlife, but invaders from outside are not the only threat that it faces. Given the wrong conditions, even a huge and long-established population can be threatened, of which there is perhaps no more appalling case than that of the American passenger pigeon. Blue and grey, with a wine red breast, it was capable of flying at up to 70 miles (110 km) an hour, and in the mid-1800s was probably the most numerous bird on Earth. It covered the forests of North America and had a population in the billions. A single flock could be up to 300 miles (480 km) long, taking days to fly by and darkening the sky as it passed. And yet, within a few decades, the passenger pigeon was extinct, wiped out by a combination of over-hunting, with tens of thousands being shot daily, and the cutting down of its native forests for agriculture. The last birds in the wild were shot in 1900 and Martha, the very last passenger pigeon, died in Cincinnati Zoo in 1914.[243] An almost unbelievable tragedy. Subject (of course) to the avoidance of unwanted unintended consequences, how lovely it would be if stored DNA could be used to enable the return of this beautiful bird.

The American Government has since taken steps to take better care of its wildlife, and in 1973 introduced the Endangered Species Act (ESA), which not only gave protection to the wildlife itself, but also to its habitat. However, if we take the example of one protected bird, the red-cockaded woodpecker, we can see that this protection has not been without its issues. This woodpecker makes its home in old pine trees, most of which are on government-owned land, but in North Carolina a good number live in trees on private land. If those trees are given legal protection, the landowner cannot fell them and sell the wood. One man, Ben Cone, calculated that the 8,000 acres (12 square miles) of land that he had inherited should have had a market value of US$1.6 million (about £1.2 million) but that, because much of it was covered with mature trees, the habitat protection afforded by the ESA meant that its actual worth was just US$260,000 (about £200,000). His reaction was to clear-cut 600 acres (1 square mile) of trees that had not yet reached maturity, in order to prevent them becoming protected as well.[244] Indeed, the National Association of House Builders has explicitly made clear to its members that, "The highest level of assurance that a property owner will not face an ESA issue is to maintain the property in a condition such that protected species cannot occupy the property."[245] Other landowners followed Ben Cone's example, thereby destroying not only the habitat of the red-cockaded woodpecker but also of much other local wildlife. In different parts of the US, the habitats of other protected birds such as the black-capped vireo, golden-cheeked warbler, northern spotted owl and the gloriously-monikered cactus ferruginous pygmy owl were similarly destroyed.[246] Some landowners have even gone down the so-called "shoot, shovel, and shut up" route, killing listed species before the authorities find out about them and take protective steps.[247]

The ESA had the stated aim that, under its protection, species would be able to recover their numbers and so be taken off the endangered list. Economist Sam Peltzman noted that, when the ESA was introduced in 1973, 119 species were listed. New species were steadily added, so that by 2003 over 1,300 were protected. However, over those 30 years, only 39 species had managed to make it off the list, but the numbers are even more disappointing than they appear. Of those 39, 15 were removed for "administrative" reasons and 9 had become extinct, whilst just 15 had recovered.[248] As another group of economists put it, there is "the distinct possibility that the Endangered Species Act is actually endangering, rather than protecting, species."[249]

In fact, it seems that the possibility of any kind of habitat protection being introduced is likely to have this sort of effect. When, in the spring of 1999, regulators in North Carolina proposed stiffer rules on draining wetlands, landowners went on a drainage and ditching spree, carrying out between 15 and 20 times the state's usual annual wetland development in just a few months.[250]

As Ben Cone's case shows, the problem from the landowners' perspective is that there is no economic upside. Once protection is in place they are prevented from managing their land as they wish, but receive no financial compensation. Sam Hamilton, former US Fish and Wildlife Service administrator for Texas, recognised this when he observed that, "The incentives are wrong here. If a rare metal is on my property the value of my land goes up. But if a rare bird is on my property the value of my property goes down."[251]

In an effort to get to grips with this issue, in the early 1990s the concept of the "Safe Harbor" was developed. This was an optional scheme for landowners, under which the Government gave them guarantees about their future use of the land. In return, the landowners pledged to improve the habitat of protected species by taking action such as drilling artificial nest cavities, removing hardwood undergrowth and allowing trees to grow for longer before being felled.

These Safe Harbor Agreements seem to have worked fairly well, and have certainly been a move in the right direction. Happily, amongst the successes has been North Carolina's red-cockaded woodpecker. Whilst under the supposed protection of the ESA, the population on private land had declined by 9% per year, but since the introduction of the Safe Harbor programme their numbers have increased, albeit only by about 1% each year in the initial 6 years.[252, 253]

As we have seen, some new inventions, such as dynamite and the

Gatling gun, were discovered to have some pretty harmful uses. But sometimes, even where the new technology itself is benign, introducing it can still have a deleterious effect. Providing fresh water for African villagers has been a perennial problem, and a device called the PlayPump seemed to provide an ingenious solution. Developed in the early 1990s, it is a child's merry-go-round, the idea being that, as children turn it as they play, underground water is pumped to a tank on the surface, thereby doing away with the laborious business of winding buckets of water up from a well. Although, at £8,700 a time (just over US$11,000 and four times the cost of installing a conventional hand-pumped well), it was fairly costly; by 2008 over 1,000 had been installed across Africa, usually replacing existing handpumps. However, as time went by it was discovered that it was not actually a terribly efficient pump and was quite heavy for children to turn. Although it had been claimed that it could provide a daily water supply for 2,500 people, it transpired that, in order to do so, it would have to be used for 27 hours a day, which is beyond the capabilities of even the most enthusiastic youngsters. In practice, adults (mainly – of course – women) have ended up doing the work, but the roundabout, being designed for children, is too low for them, and is harder (and rather more undignified) than the hand-pumping that they did before. Some users in Mozambique reported that the time which they spent pumping water had gone from three-quarters of an hour to almost two hours. And with many of the PlayPumps breaking down and taking months to be mended, many villagers were forced to travel to the next village to fetch their water, thus taking even more time and also irritating their neighbours in the process. Sadly, the introduction of the PlayPump has left many people having to work harder for their water, or even being left with none at all.[254, 255]

One genuinely labour-saving device that still had dreadful ramifications was the cotton gin, invented by Eli Whitney in

1793. Until that time, growing cotton in the US had been too expensive to be worthwhile, as the only variety that would grow there was short staple cotton, and so much cost and effort was required to remove the sticky seeds by hand that it was very expensive, even with the use of slave labour. However, by mechanising the process, the new machine was capable of cleaning up to 50 pounds (68 kg) of cotton each day without the need for manual labourers, whether paid or slaves. This was good news for the landowners, but turned out to be very bad news for the slaves. Whilst not required to clean the cotton, it still had to be hand-picked, and slave labour was very viable indeed for that. The first United States Census revealed that in 1790 there were almost 700,000 slaves in America, but the demand for free cotton picking labour was such that, by the time that the Civil War broke out in 1861, that number had more than quintupled to almost 4 million.

Economically, cotton became an enormous success. It was the world's most traded commodity, and two-thirds of it was produced in America. But although Eli Whitney's invention was extremely beneficial to some American landowners, it brought a miserable life for the millions of ordinary people who were forced into slavery. And as if that horror wasn't enough in itself, the arguments between the North and South over the keeping of slaves eventually exploded into the American Civil War, in which more American soldiers died than in both World Wars combined.[256] And Eli Whitney himself had no particular reason to rejoice in his invention because, due to various patent issues, his earnings from it barely covered his costs.

Perhaps those striving to bring about scientific progress could do worse than consider some form of Nobel laureate Joseph Rotblat's Hippocratic oath for graduating scientists:

I promise to work for a better world, where science and technology are used in socially responsible ways. I will not use my education for

*any purpose intended to harm human beings or the environment...
I will consider the ethical implications of my work before I take
action.*

with perhaps the addition of something along the lines of

*... and I will endeavour to take into account any unintended
harmful consequences that my work may be put to.*[257]

However, even adhering to that oath would probably not
have protected a number of other people who have had very
personal reasons to regret their inventions. Earlier, we met with
Thomas Midgley, the man who put the first CFC into fridges
by replacing the toxic ammonia with a gas that turned out to
be environmentally lethal. He contracted polio a few years later
and, finding himself bed-bound, invented a complicated system
of pulleys to help him get out of bed. Tragically, he became
entangled in it and was strangled by his own invention. In 1863,
poor William Bullock invented a version of the rotary printing
press, but 4 years later caught his leg in its gears and died as a
result. Other inventions seem more obviously dangerous. Francis
Stanley was killed in 1918 when driving a Stanley Steamer, the
car he had invented, which overturned after crashing into a
woodpile. But perhaps most tragically, Marie Curie, the only
person to have been awarded a Nobel Prize in two different
sciences, died of leukaemia in 1934 as a direct result of her
experiments with radioactive substances.

If one wishes to avoid coming to harm through one's own
invention, it would be wise to steer well clear of the world of
aviation, which (understandably) is littered with casualties.
Amongst those who have fallen foul of their own inventions
is Frenchman Jean-François Pilâtre de Rozier, who in the late
18th century constructed the Rozière balloon, only to die when it
crashed as he was attempting to fly across the English Channel.

In 1912 Franz Reichelt fell to his death from the first tier of the Eiffel Tower whilst testing his "coat parachute", whilst in 1973 Henry Smolinski and Hal Blake both died when the AVE Mizar, a car-cum-aeroplane that they pioneered, crashed during a test flight after its wings detached.

* The term seems to originate in German economist Horst Siebert's 2001 book *Der Kobra-Effekt*, but it is unclear whether the episode actually happened quite like this.

Chapter 6

Surely trying to protect people can't be bad?

Much (but often unfairly) maligned, the intention of "Health and Safety" legislation is self-evidently to keep us from harm. But even if we may grumble that we are being mollycoddled on occasion, we can presumably rest assured that at least we are being protected? Once again, not necessarily. But how could efforts to improve health and safety not be a good thing?

Earlier we looked at some of the dangers of trying to protect people by banning alcohol or dangerous drugs. Another much less restricted substance, tobacco, has been a major industry for a considerable time, and was in fact once lauded for its claimed health-giving properties. Now, however, we are only too aware that, by combining highly addictive elements with over 60 cancer-causing chemicals, tobacco is at best unhealthy and, at worst, lethal. In fact, it is reckoned that smoking causes almost 80,000 deaths per year in the UK,[258] almost half a million per year in the US[259] and, that worldwide, more than 7 million people die every year from its effects. And that ignores the chronic but non-fatal illnesses that affect many more millions as a result of smoking.[260]

However, although governments have taken ever more punitive action on smoking, they have almost without exception stopped short of imposing an outright tobacco ban. Indeed, to date, only one country has attempted to do so. This is the tiny Kingdom of Bhutan, nestling in the Himalayas, which in 2004 introduced laws prohibiting the sale of tobacco products (although some very highly taxed imports are still permitted). One, entirely predictable, result is that the smuggling of cigarettes into the country from nearby India has become a major problem, with cigarettes selling on the Bhutan black market at three times their original price.[261]

Governments elsewhere have tended to adopt a more multi-pronged approach to reducing the harm caused by tobacco smoking. The UK Government has run awareness campaigns to alert smokers to the dangers, has banned cigarette advertising and has forced manufacturers both to include warnings on packs and make the packaging as unappealing as possible. Legislation has been introduced to ban smoking in public places and on public transport, whilst retailers have been forced to hide tobacco products from view in order to shield them from children and help adults to resist temptation. At the same time, smokers have been hit in the pocket by steady increases in tobacco taxes and duties.

This last option is one that governments throughout the ages have found appealing, as it reassures the public that this is being treated as a serious issue whilst (because the rate at which smoking falls tends to be less than the rate at which the tax is increased) boosting the government's income. No sooner had tobacco appeared in Britain than Queen Elizabeth I was slapping a tax on it – of 2 pence per pound (about 450 grams), but her successor James I, who strongly disapproved of smoking, multiplied that tax forty-fold, increasing it to 6 shillings and 8 pence. Today, for every £9 (US$12) pack of 20 cigarettes that is bought in the UK, about £6.50 (US$8.50) goes to the Government, which equates to about £200 (US$260) in taxes and duties on a pound of tobacco, more than twice the punitive tax imposed by James I after allowing for inflation over that time. In 2015/16, smokers coughed up an impressive £12 billion (about US$16 billion) to the UK Exchequer,[262] thereby saving taxpayers 2p on the basic rate of income tax, although smokers also cost the overall economy an estimated £12.9 billion (about US$16.8 billion) per year in NHS costs and lost productivity, so smoking actually ends up as a lose-lose activity.[263, 264] However, as the price spirals ever higher, the result is an effective ban for poorer people, as they simply become unable to afford to buy cigarettes. Consequently, there is increased smuggling of cigarettes from countries where duty is lower, and the proliferation of bootleg (and potentially more dangerous) cigarettes. If the Government pushes the cost too high, its income will fall, criminal behaviour will increase and smokers will be put at greater danger. And this is already happening. In 2016, an HMRC spokesman reported that over 3.5 billion illicit cigarettes and 599 tonnes (660 US tons) of hand-rolling tobacco had been seized in the last two years.[265] And this total naturally takes no account of the illicit tobacco that isn't intercepted.

Another approach is to encourage smokers to move to less dangerous products such as e-cigarettes, which have provided an alternative to tobacco for those who want to stay healthier whilst still enjoying their hit of nicotine. This seems to be having some effect and, by 2015 in the UK, about 4% of adults had taken to these, which is credited with a fall of nearly 3 percentage points in those smoking tobacco, down from 20.1% of adults in 2010 to 17.2% in 2015.[266]

Back in the 1950s, as the association between smoking and cancer became more apparent, manufacturers became keen to produce "safer" cigarettes. First came filters, followed by "light" and "low-tar" products. By switching to these supposedly less risky products, smokers were led to believe that they could continue to enjoy their habit more safely. So effective were the campaigns that by 1960, more than half of smokers had switched to filtered cigarettes[267] and by the 2010s, over 90% of cigarettes sold were filters.[268] However, by the mid-1960s manufacturers realised that the problem with cigarettes is that the stuff that is harmful in the smoke produced by cigarettes and the stuff which provides the smoker with "satisfaction" are essentially one and the same.[269] The filter mixes air with the smoke so that, with each drag, the smoker receives a lot of air and much less smoke, and so less tar and nicotine. But the smoker's body craves the same amount of nicotine, and so she compensates by smoking more and taking longer puffs in order to get the same "hit". In doing so, the harmful tars and chemicals are pulled deeper into the lungs.[270]

Smokers trying to do the healthy thing were in fact doing the opposite, as a 1992 editorial in the *American Journal of Public Health* stressed, stating that "the existence of low tar/nicotine cigarettes has actually caused more smoking than would have occurred in their absence and thereby raised the morbidity and mortality associated with smoking."[271] In 2003 the EU took legislative action, banning any cigarettes which claimed to be "mild", "light" or "low tar", and the US followed suit in 2010.

If all else fails, it is a very real temptation to point out to smoking friends or relations the dangers of their habit and implore them to just give up. But, as we saw earlier, ordering people about can be counterproductive, and telling them not to smoke can have a similar effect. Thus, the 1999 "Talk: They'll Listen" campaign, which encouraged parents to make it clear to their children that they shouldn't smoke, actually resulted in 15 to 17 year olds becoming somewhat *more* likely to smoke. The cynic might note that the programme was instigated by tobacco company Philip Morris, who perhaps suspected what the outcome might be.[272]

Along with smoking and drinking, being overweight is something of a red-flag to health professionals. For those who qualify as obese (which, astonishingly, is a quarter of UK adults), the consequences can include developing Type 2 diabetes, heart disease, cancers and a greater likelihood of strokes. It is estimated that obesity reduces life expectancy by an average of 3 to 10 years, depending on its severity, and accounts for at least 1 in every 13 deaths in Europe.[273] However, as with smoking (and so many other bad habits), attempting to encourage people to lose weight by pointing out the negative effects may be a self-defeating exercise. In a 2014 study in the *Journal of Experimental Social Psychology*,[274] a group of women were asked to read and summarise either an article suggesting that overweight people find it harder to get jobs or an article making the same point about smokers. Afterwards, the group was given a break in a room in which there were bowls filled with M&Ms and the like. Those women who thought of themselves as overweight and read the article about overweight people consumed about 80 calories *more* on average than similar women who had read the smoking article. It seems that, having felt stigmatised by what they read, they became anxious, which they dealt with by eating. Contrarily, women who didn't feel overweight had had their sense of self-control reinforced by the weight article and consequently ate less. As journalist Oliver Burkeman has wryly observed, this is why slim people shouldn't design anti-obesity campaigns, as what has one effect on the slim can have just the opposite effect on the overweight people that they are trying to influence.[275]

So we need to be very careful when pointing out to people their lifestyle deficiencies. But let us suppose that somehow someone has got the message and has embarked on a beneficial course of action. Perhaps they have wisely begun to resist those M&Ms or started taking a brisk 10-minute daily walk. Surely they are on a path that will lead to a better life? However (and there's that wretched "however" again...), it turns out that even when we are doing exactly the right thing, this can have repercussions. There is a likelihood that by doing so, we will subconsciously give ourselves permission to compensate for it elsewhere. It's called "moral licensing", and means that if, for example, people are given vitamin pills (or even placebos masquerading as vitamin pills), they will tend to exercise less, eat less healthily and indulge in riskier behaviour. In one study, smokers who were given vitamin pills became more likely to light up immediately afterwards, and even (bizarrely) to feel that they were less liable to be the victim of an accident![276] In another experiment, people being asked to sample and review oatmeal cookies helped themselves to 35% more when the health benefits of the cookies were emphasised.[277]

By engaging in a "healthy" activity (or even just believing that we are), we open ourselves up to the very real possibility that any gain will be offset or even reversed by "treats" that we allow ourselves or by the greater risks that we consequently feel we are able to take with our health. Indeed, from personal experience, I admit to having found it much harder to resist the lure of a bar of chocolate on the day after playing a nice healthy game of football.

But it's not just people who need to be kept healthy. By 2013, concern over the incidence of tuberculosis in UK cattle had reached new heights. Bovine TB is a continual source of fear to farmers, as it means the destruction of any infected animals and the whole farm being quarantined until all danger of contamination has passed. The Government recompenses farmers for their losses, but in 2012, 28,000 cattle had been slaughtered at a cost of £100 million (about US$130 million) to taxpayers. The finger of blame had been pointed at badgers, who can suffer from a form of TB which it was thought was passed on to cows. As a result, the UK Government introduced an experimental cull of badgers, intending to destroy 70% of badgers in the affected area of Somerset and so remove the threat to cattle. However, killing badgers is a difficult and laborious process. It was decided that the most efficient and humane course of action was to shoot the badgers at night. But at the end of the six-week cull it was reckoned that, of an estimated 3,000 badgers, fewer than 800 (about 25%) had been killed. As with the pigs in America, one of the problems with firing guns at badgers is that the badgers who are not shot run off as quickly as they can. In so doing, they spread the disease more widely. As the shadow environment secretary Mary Creagh observed: "We are now facing the worst case scenario: badgers have been killed, TB in cattle may well get worse and we are no closer to tackling this terrible disease." As the culls continued into the autumn of 2015, the number of herds of cows in Dorset suffering TB outbreaks rose from 14 before the cull to 18 afterwards. On the edge of the cull area matters were even worse, with 3 outbreaks before the cull, but 8 afterwards[278] and the total number of cattle slaughtered in Dorset over a 12-month period increased from 762 to 1,077, a rise of over 40%.[279] A further cull took place in Gloucestershire in 2015, with the result that the number of cattle put down because of Bovine TB in the county increased by almost 16% over the year.[280] If shooting badgers has an effect on TB in cattle, it seems to be that it makes it worse rather than better.

So, if improving health isn't quite as easy as we might have imagined, how about keeping safe?

One instance that shows just how carefully you need to think through your plans for keeping people safe occurred at the end of the 2015/16 English football season. As the Manchester United and Bournemouth teams were warming up on the pitch, a mobile phone was found suspiciously taped to a gas pipe in toilets in the stadium. The ground was quickly evacuated and the match abandoned, before the Bomb Disposal Unit carried out a controlled explosion on the suspect device. However, it turned out to be no more than a dummy bomb which had been accidentally left behind after a security training exercise for sniffer dogs.[281]

Mercifully, this incident resulted in no injury (other than to the reputation of the company carrying out the exercise), and we can see how, with a bit of basic double checking, it could have been avoided. But to illustrate further how it is possible to take ill-conceived safety precautions, we turn to the nuclear power industry. Now nobody wants to have a nuclear reactor going wrong. And so, when in the late 1950s, the Fermi nuclear plant was being built just 29 miles (47 km) to the south of Detroit, the American Nuclear Regulatory Commission kept a very close eye on its construction. Overheating of the reactor was a major concern and so the core of the reactor was to be cooled by a flow of liquid sodium. The Commission insisted that pie-shaped flow guides with zirconium filters were installed to ensure that the sodium flowed properly in the event of a meltdown. However, in October 1966, as the plant was being brought into full operation, that was what almost happened, as the reactor core suffered a partial meltdown, threatening the population of Detroit. Disaster was averted, although the plant remained closed for 4 years. The subsequent inquiry eventually discovered that the problem was that a blockage had stopped one of the tanks draining. After many efforts, workers finally managed to insert a robotic arm into the tank to retrieve the material causing the problem. On examination, they discovered that it was the remains of one of the zirconium filters, which had broken off and obstructed the cooling flow through some of the fuel elements. As David Lochbaum, of the Union of Concerned Scientists, put it, "A feature installed late in the reactor's design intended to provide better protection in event of a meltdown triggered a meltdown."[282, 283]

Thirteen years later there was another major incident at an American nuclear power plant, this time at Three Mile Island, near Harrisburg, the state capital of Pennsylvania. Once again, unintended consequences were to the fore. A relatively minor malfunction in a cooling circuit got out of control, in part because the operators were unable to diagnose the problem. By the time they found out what had gone wrong, almost half of the uranium core in one of the reactors had melted, destroying the reactor. Bringing the situation under control was hampered by the way in which the operators in the control room were alerted to the initial problem. As Edward Frederick, one of the operators on duty that day, later told a New York Court, "In the first few minutes after the accident, 400 to 500 alarm lights lit up on the control panel and 300 to 400 other panel indicators showed that something was going wrong."[284] And whilst a red light indicated an open valve or active equipment and a green indicated a closed valve or inactive equipment, in the ordinary course of business some lights were supposed to be red and some green, so it was impossible for even a highly trained operator to quickly see where the problems were. To make things even more difficult, whilst they were trying to work out what was going on, there was a cacophony of over 100 different alarms shrieking in the control room. As Philippe Jamet, head of nuclear installation safety at the International Atomic Energy Agency, has said, "The people who were operating the plant, they were absolutely, completely lost."[285]

One of the ways in which you are most likely to die unintentionally is in a road traffic accident, and since the advent of the motor car, governments have been trying to reduce the number of people that they kill. When the car was a newfangled thing, drivers were forced to have someone walk ahead of their vehicles whilst carrying a red flag in order to warn other road users of their approach. It may be just as well that this is no longer the case, although often in a city like London traffic doesn't need the red flag person to keep it to walking pace. In 1930 a UK speed limit of 30 mph was introduced in built-up areas, and since then more and more legislation has had the aim of cutting the number of road deaths. Over the last 80 years, the number of cars and distance driven has increased exponentially. In 1938 (the first year for which records are available), there were about 1.5 million vehicles on the road, covering a total of 29 billion miles (47 billion km) each year. By 2014 there were over 20 times as many cars (35.6 million) covering 311 billion miles (500 billion km).[286*] To put that into some context, there are now about the same number of Ford Focuses driving around the UK as the total number of cars in 1938. The efforts to improve road safety have been startlingly successful. Despite the extraordinary increase in road use, UK road deaths have actually dropped by almost two-thirds over the last 90 years, falling from 6,648 in 1938 to 1,775 in 2014 (having peaked at 10,073 in 1940 when blackouts were in force).[287] The fatality rate per billion vehicle miles (bvm) driven has fallen almost every year from a peak of 165 deaths per bvm in 1949 to 5.7 deaths in 2014.

However, not every safety measure has been entirely beneficial. For example, whilst the compulsory wearing of seat belts in cars (introduced in the UK in 1983) has undoubtedly saved many lives and prevented injuries for those involved in accidents, there is compelling evidence to suggest that wearing a seat belt and driving a car fitted with all the latest safety features may, by making the driver feel safer, encourage them to engage in riskier behaviour.

In the 1980s an experiment was carried out to test this hypothesis. Participants were separated into two groups and asked to drive go-karts, with one group wearing seat belts and the other not. When the groups were swapped around, it was found that drivers who went from unbelted to belted then drove consistently faster.[288**] Another study conducted on roads in the Netherlands showed that when non-users of seatbelts belted up, they tended to drive faster, change lanes at higher speed, brake more dangerously and be more likely to tailgate.[289]

Their behaviour may be explained by the idea of "Risk Homeostasis", which suggests that drivers unconsciously seek to maintain a certain level of hazard. The safer we feel, the riskier our driving is likely to become. However, whilst those in the cars benefit from their new-found safety features, any pedestrian or cyclist that they may plough into has no such protection and is more likely to be injured or killed. Thus, in 2014, car occupants themselves only accounted for fewer than half (47%) of road deaths, with pedestrians contributing 26%, pedal cyclists 7% and motorcyclists 20%.[290] Indeed, in his letter to *The Scotsman* newspaper, Stanley McWhirter probably spoke for many when he wrote that, "It would help if seat belts for drivers were banned, and the air-bag was replaced with a sharp spike pointing towards the driver's face. The result would be that drivers would take active measures to improve their driving to avoid all crashes."[291]

Whilst not going quite that far, some researchers have suggested that a move in this direction might actually be worth considering. Dutchman Hans Monderman felt that removing zebra crossings, signs, traffic lights and even road markings might lead to fewer, and less serious, accidents. His theory was that, by introducing uncertainty into the minds of drivers, they would be kept more alert and their speed nudged down.[292]**** Being encouraged to make eye contact with other road users should mean that they would interact with them much more safely. Experiments were carried out in towns in the northern Friesland area of the Netherlands, replacing traffic lights at dangerous junctions with a tree in the middle of the road. The result was that, whereas previously 2 or 3 pedestrians had been killed each year, the death rate dropped to nil.[293] Canadians have in fact been doing something along these lines for many years, as there is often no automatic right of way at Canadian crossroads, so that road users are forced to agree between themselves who is going to go first. In Britain, there have been experiments along the same lines. In April 2004 the village of Seend in Wiltshire removed all white lines from its roads, with the result that accidents fell by a third and speed was reduced by an average of 5%.[294] In the city of Brighton in East Sussex, planners expanded this approach to deal with an especially problematic road. Despite being home to Brighton's magnificent Theatre Royal, New Road's problems had been summed up in damning terms by urban designer David Rudlin, "One side was lined with magnificent Regency buildings, the other by the brooding presence of the Pavilion... It felt like a bit of High Street cut off from the surrounding street network and relegated to the role of a back street, with all the attendant menace and seediness that implies."[295] It was decided to turn the road into a "shared space", with benches installed and road markings removed, so that pedestrians, cyclists and drivers all had to work with each other. When the road was reopened in 2007 it quickly achieved its objectives. A survey a year later showed that pedestrian activity had risen 162% and cycling 22%, whilst traffic had fallen by 93%. A safety audit stated that, "Motorists appear to behave as though they are intruders in the street; give almost total priority to pedestrians and most drive at the lowest possible speeds."[296] 80% of New Road businesses feel that the scheme has had a beneficial impact, not just financially, but on the general well-being of residents.[297]

In the summer of 1910, a series of forest fires broke out across the north-western US states of Idaho, Montana and Washington. The Forest Service just about managed to keep them under control until 20th August, when hurricane-force winds swept across the region, fanning the embers back to life across the whole of the Northern Rockies. Forester Edward G. Stahl recalled seeing "flames hundreds of feet high, fanned by a tornadic wind so violent that the flames flattened out ahead, swooping to earth in great darting curves, truly a veritable red demon from hell." The power of the fire was such that huge trees were sucked from the ground, roots and all, and hurled through the air.[298] More than 3 million acres (about 4,700 square miles and equivalent to an area about two-thirds of the size of Wales) had been burnt, 85 people died and a number of towns were destroyed. Smoke from the fire reached New England, over 2,000 miles (3,200 km) away, whilst soot travelled all the way to Greenland, almost 3,000 miles (4,800 km).[299] In the years that followed, further fires were a regular occurrence, and so in 1935, the United States Forest Service gave very strict instructions that any fires were to be extinguished as soon as possible, in fact specifically, to "Put out every forest fire

by 10am on the morning after the day when it is first reported."
This policy, accompanied by new fire-fighting technology and
more roads (enabling fire engines to reach fires more quickly),
seemed very successful. The area burned by wildland fires fell
from 30 million acres (almost 47,000 square miles or about the
area of Greece) per year in the 1930s to between 2 and 5 million
acres (3,000 to 8,000 square miles) a year by the 1960s.[300]

However, since then, the picture has changed. Today
wildfires, on average, burn twice as much land every year as they
did 40 years ago. More worryingly, since 2005 there has been an
average of 10 so-called "megafires" each year.[301] These are fires
that burn at least 100,000 acres (150 square miles), although they
can be much more extensive. In August 2004 the Taylor Complex
Fire burned for over a month in Alaska, burning more than 1.3
million acres (over 2,000 square miles), just one of a series of fires
in the state that summer that razed over 6.6 million acres (over
10,000 square miles). It was the worst year for fires in Alaska
since records began, as was the case in 2014 in Washington State,
when the largest fire in its history swept across the slopes of the
Cascade Range, destroying more than 250,000 acres (almost 400
square miles), and at its fiercest devouring forest at what the
National Geographic understandably described as the "hypersonic
pace" of 3.8 acres (over 18,000 square yards) per second.

Research has shown that there are a number of contributory
factors to this surge in wildfires, one of which turns out to be
the aggressive fire control policy of the US Forest Service. Tree
records show that historically, any area of forest would be subject
to a forest fire set off by lightning about once every ten years,
but that these tended to be fairly minor in scale. The regularity
of the fires meant that an understory of Douglas Fir seedlings
would begin to grow, reaching about 20 feet high in the 10 years,
only to be devoured by the next fire. However, the main tree
of the forest, the Ponderosa Pine, has an extraordinarily thick,
2-inch bark, and grows to over 200 feet in height, so they came

through these fires relatively unscathed. However, once the policy of extinguishing small fires came into effect, the Douglas Fir saplings were able to grow much bigger and create a very dense understory, so that when, inevitably, a fire broke out that couldn't be quickly extinguished, the Douglas Fir saplings were tall enough to provide a ladder to allow the fire to jump into the Ponderosa crowns. As author and ecologist Jared Diamond has written, "The outcome is sometimes an unstoppable inferno in which flames shoot 400 feet into the air, leap from crown to crown across wide gaps, reach temperatures of 2,000 degrees Fahrenheit, kill the tree seed bank in the soil and may be followed by mudslides and mass erosion. Foresters now identify the biggest problem in managing western forests as what to do with those increased fuel loads that built up during the previous half-century of effective fire suppression."[302] This strategy has also been applied throughout the temperate forests of Australia, Canada and the Mediterranean. If the old trees of British Columbia in Canada are examined, blackened tree rings reveal that, up to the end of the 19th century, they were being singed every 10 to 40 years. The policy of suppressing those fires has meant that the fire services have steadily been building up huge stockpiles of kindling in the forests. The result is that, as David Bowman a fire scientist at the University of Tasmania has graphically put it, "Globally we have been feeding the monster and now the monster is feeding itself. Slaying this monster will be difficult."[303]

There is now a realisation, both in the US and elsewhere, that fire management tactics must change, for as Professor David Martell of the Forestry Faculty at Ontario's University of Toronto has pointed out, "Fire is a natural part of forest ecosystems in Canada. When you burn, you're recycling nutrients and improving the habitat for animals... But in general, fire is natural, fire is good for trees in the long run. I always say to my students: Fire destroys trees, it doesn't destroy forests."[304]

Megafires are of course an exception to this rule, and a lot more money has been allocated to try to deal with them, with the US fire-fighting budget quintupling from US$600 million (about £460 million) in 1995 to US$3 billion (about £2.3 billion) per year by 2014, with the actual spend frequently exceeding those figures. However, having allowed the understory to grow unchecked for so many years, Jared Diamond estimates that to clear it now from the 100 million acres (about 150,000 square miles) of western US forests would amount to a staggering US$100 billion (about £77 billion).

Concern for health and safety is clearly a good thing – road safety has improved dramatically over the years, and no one would wish for a return to a time when, for example, builders developed asbestosis from demolishing buildings. Bartenders' lungs must appreciate not being exposed to "secondary" smoke in pubs, and in the 40 years since the introduction of the Health and Safety at Work Act in 1974, fatal injuries to UK employees have fallen by 87%, whilst reported non-fatal injuries have dropped by over 70%.[305] However, as we again have seen, trying to make things better can still rebound on us.

Giving up a harmful habit is going to be beneficial but is usually difficult. With smoking, there are a number of pathways. Smokers can replace their cigarettes with something else that gives them the same nicotine "hit" such as a patch or an e-cigarette. They would be advised to avoid situations which trigger their cigarette craving and try using distraction tactics when their need for a cigarette is strongest. The most effective way seems to be just to go cold turkey – making the decision not to smoke again and following through on that promise, whilst others steadily reduce the number of cigarettes that they smoke each day. However, all of these have to be driven by the smoker's own desire to stop. As we've seen, having other people telling you what to do can have just the opposite effect, and even helpfully giving people information can backfire. If smokers feel that other people are judging, scolding or nagging them, this is likely to make them feel worse about themselves and thus more likely to turn to a cigarette to make themselves feel better.

Doctor Max Pemberton, a smoker himself into his 30s, had found that no matter how he tried, he couldn't give up the habit, despite being a doctor and all too aware of the health risks. Intellectually he knew that it was bad for him, but as he has said, the thought of giving up made him feel profoundly sad. He had tried patches, pills, gum, sprays and books, but not only had they not helped, some (we may not at this point be shocked to learn) actually resulted in him smoking more. After the death from lung cancer of two close relatives, he grasped the nettle and realised that he ought to try a technique that he had used successfully with drug addicts. Pemberton knew that people tend to smoke despite their misgivings about it, creating a mental conflict, or "cognitive dissonance" as psychologists label it. He attempted to deal with this by drawing up a list of all the things that he really liked about smoking. As he said, if it didn't give you something, surely you wouldn't do it? Then he wrote a list of all the things that stopped him from giving up. Thirdly, he wrote a list of all the benefits that giving up would bring. He points out that all of the apparent benefits of smoking are in fact illusory. The cognitive dissonance that we feel leads our mind to come up with "cognitive distortions", arguments that are apparently logical, but which, when examined carefully, fall apart. He highlights the so-called ability of nicotine to relieve stress. In fact, because nicotine doesn't stay in the body for very long, smokers spend their days in a constant state of mild withdrawal, and in fact smoking actually raises blood pressure and heart rate, which can make stress worse. All smoking is doing is momentarily relieving the smoker's nicotine withdrawal symptoms. The final stage is to present the evidence, as though to a judge and jury, making the defence's case for continuing to smoke as strongly as you can. Then, switch sides and present the case for the prosecution, pointing out all the flaws in the defence's argument. Hopefully, the result will be (as it was for Max Pemberton) that by spelling out the argument in an objective way, you provide yourself with the ammunition that you need when next tempted by a cigarette.[306]

Interestingly, he also warns that criticism, coercion and even the receipt of seemingly helpful advice from non-smokers (as with the slim trying to help the overweight) can often be counterproductive. So, if you have a friend or family member who seems to have some sort of issue, whether smoking, weight or perhaps hoarding or some other unhealthy lifestyle, it seems that the best course that you can adopt is to be an encourager and help them to objectively resolve their problems themselves. And if you yourself happen to have some besetting temptation with which you ineffectively struggle (and which of us doesn't?), exposing it to the light of some forensic cross-examination may be well worth trying.

* And interesting to note that each car is now driven only half as far as in 1938.

** Although those going from belted to unbelted didn't drive slower – perhaps because they had already navigated the course safely once?

*** Although uncertainty on the road may not always be a good thing. Whilst on holiday in France a few years ago, my family and I watched bemusedly at a set of traffic lights that had gone to "flashing amber" mode for all drivers at off-peak times. To us, this seemed to be telling all drivers that they had right of way, and indeed, it was only a few minutes before one car, travelling at some speed, hit another crossing at right angles to it.

Chapter 7

Can bad intentions turn out for the good?

We've seen how, time after time, good intentions can go wrong, but happily, the same can apply to bad intentions as well.

In the early 1940s, continental Europe had fallen to Nazism, and Britain stood alone. Subject to constant bombing and upheavals of every kind and extremely fearful for the future, this was not a good time for the country. On top of the usual horrors of wartime, Britons quickly began to get hungry. In peacetime, Britain had imported two-thirds of its food, but attacks on shipping quickly reduced those imports from 55 million tons per year to 12 million,[307] so that many everyday commodities ran short. In January 1940, in an attempt to ensure that everyone received their fair share (and in the face of much opposition from the press), the Government introduced food rationing.

To run the scheme, they brought in an outsider, a successful businessman, Fred Marquis, and appointed him Minister of Food. Marquis came from a poor background and had had a neighbour who had died from malnutrition, and he was determined to turn this problem into an opportunity to improve the health of the nation. He quickly assembled a team– including a professor of biochemistry, the President of the Royal Society and the Minister of Agriculture – and "worked out a diet for the nation that would supply all the calories and all the vitamins that were needed for different age groups, for the fighting services, for the heavy manual workers, for the ordinary housewife, for the babies and children and for the pregnant and nursing mothers."[308]

The food was rationed out accordingly, and although it changed from time to time, a typical weekly adult allowance would have been a mere 2 oz (56 g) each of butter, cheese, margarine, cooking fat and tea or coffee; 4 oz (113 g) of jam or other preserve; 4 oz (113 g) of bacon; 12 oz (340 g) of sugar and meat; 1 egg; and 2 pints (just over 1 litre) of milk. This enforced diet wasn't a short-term one either, with rationing in force not only during the remainder of the war, but continuing in one form or another for a total of 14 years, an almost inconceivable privation today.

When added to the inevitable stress of the war, it might be expected that the nation's health would suffer. The outcome, however, was just the opposite, and a remarkable triumph for Fred Marquis. Rationing actually improved the diet of poorer people by increasing their protein and vitamins and reducing the amount of fats and sugar in their diet.[309] As William Sitwell, Marquis' biographer, states: "Britain, at the end of the war, was not just in good physical shape, it had – and has never been – so healthy... Child mortality had never been so low, and far fewer mothers died in childbirth. Fewer babies had been stillborn and children were both taller and sturdier."[310] Deaths from natural causes dropped, and even tooth decay had been reduced. There were falls in the incidence of heart disease, type 2 diabetes, high blood pressure and certain cancers.[311] And this was all achieved with fewer doctors and other health professionals, most of whom had been deployed overseas as part of the war effort.

Nazi Germany had inadvertently provided Britain with an effective way of improving the nation's health.

Even without the benign assistance of a Fred Marquis, there is evidence to suggest that times of austerity, such as that brought about by the 2008 financial crash, may improve people's health. Iceland is a case in point. In early October 2008 the entire country was swaying on the brink of bankruptcy. Over a matter of a few months, the three largest commercial banks had failed, the stock market had lost 95% of its value, the currency had collapsed and the interest rate on loans had soared to over 300%. The result was that almost all businesses on the island went bankrupt and one-sixth of the population lost their entire savings. However, people were forced to improve their lifestyle. Imports became prohibitively expensive, and although fewer fruit and vegetables were eaten, this was more than offset by reductions in smoking and the consumption of alcohol, soft drinks and sweets. People could no longer afford harmful indoor tanning sessions, and were even benefitting from more sleep.[312]

In Arizona in the early 1990s, one group of people voluntarily agreed to undergo these sorts of privations. "Biosphere 2" was a sealed environment covering about 3 acres (about 12,000 square metres) (somewhat like a less elegant Eden Project), which mimicked the conditions in which a colony in outer-space might find itself. A group of eight bioscientists was locked in for two years whilst they attempted to survive on what they could grow themselves. Their restricted diet led to a general improvement in the health of the participants, their cholesterol and blood pressure was lowered and their immune systems enhanced.[313]

Workers on the London Underground have also done their unwitting bit to improve people's health. In the climax to a long-running dispute, in 2014 a series of strikes shut down much of the London Underground network. During one 48-hour strike, three lines were completely shut, with reduced service on other lines, and almost 2/3 of stations were closed for at least part of the time. With well over 4 million journeys being taken on a typical day, Londoners were badly affected, but a study of commuters affected by the strike has shown some intriguing results. As travellers were forced to find alternative routes to work it was found that 5% found a better route, which they stuck to once the strike was over. Their commute became speedier, more pleasant, and/or just healthier, and at the same time improved the journey for people on the routes that they had abandoned. According to BBC reports, commuter Chris Fry abandoned public transport altogether for part of his journey, having discovered that, "The walk from Liverpool Street was a refreshing change from the horrors of the Circle Line. I suspect I may permanently switch

so I can cut out this, the most stressful part of my journey."[314]
On average, a full 40 seconds had been shaved off the average
commute time, which may not sound very exciting for an
individual, but multiplied by the millions who travel in London
means that over 40,000 hours of extra time has been freed up
every day.[315] Of course, partially closing the Tube network is
a somewhat radical way of achieving efficiency savings, but
Transport for London is now helping travellers to make better
choices, and is for example displaying maps indicating how long
it takes to walk between stations.

Despite the efforts of the 2008 crash and London Underground
workers, UK obesity rates have still tripled over the last 30
years[316] whilst cases of type 2 diabetes are at an all-time high. It
seems rather a pity that on the whole we seem to be unwilling
to eat healthily unless we are forced to, but with the current
popularity of "choice", attempts at forcing people to become
healthier by reducing their choices is going to be a difficult sell
under normal circumstances.

Throughout history, oppression has often had the opposite effect
to that intended, and has proved the truth of Tertullian's saying
that, "The blood of the martyrs is the seed of the Church."[317]
In the first and second centuries CE, Christians went through
periods of ruthless persecution by the Roman authorities, being
expelled by Claudius from Rome in 49CE and from Jerusalem
in about 135CE. But rather than killing off the new religion, this
enforced dispersal resulted in its spread throughout the whole
of the Roman Empire.

Violence against those who are seen as being threatening
(for whatever reason) continues to be virulent today. Malala
Yousafzai could certainly attest to that. Having campaigned from
a young age for the rights of Pakistani girls to be educated, she
upset the Taliban so much that, in October 2012, they attempted
to murder the 15-year-old girl as she travelled home from school.

But, after weeks in intensive care, she survived, and the attack backfired spectacularly. In the year following the attempt on her life, the local government increased spending on education and enrolled an additional 75,000 girls into schools.[318] Such has been the effect of her message that her 16th birthday was designated worldwide "Malala Day" by the United Nations, and she was the co-recipient of the 2014 Nobel Peace Prize. As she has pointed out, "The Taliban shot me to silence me – instead, the whole world is listening to my message now."[319]

Sometimes even self-inflicted damage can have a surprisingly beneficial outcome. Justine Roberts, a co-founder of the Mumsnet website, has said that, "Sometimes what seems like the worst of times is, in fact, a blessing. Mumsnet was catapulted into the mainstream by Gina Ford, strict parenting guru and author of *The Contented Little Baby Book*. She sued us for libel and tried to shut us down by threatening our Internet service provider, after Mumsnet users posted allegedly defamatory comments about her... It was a nightmare at the time, but from a few years distance, I recognise that she did more to promote our website than any amount of advertising could have done."[320]

Chapter 8

The upside – unlooked for benefits

Even better than having a negative turn into a positive, there have been occasions when good intentions have not only achieved the desired result but have also brought about an unexpectedly beneficial side effect.

In 1800 the River Thames was clean enough for salmon to be commercially fished. However, by the mid-1830s, London's soaring population meant that sewage could no longer be transported out of the city. The combination of 200,000 cesspits and the newfangled flushing toilets, most of which emptied into the Thames, polluted the river and resulted in an appalling stench.[321] The situation steadily worsened over the years, but the summer of 1858 was particularly hot, with temperatures of over 30°C (86°F), and the heat caused the waste that had been poured into the river over the years to ferment, leading to what became known as the Great Stink. As the stench increased, the Houses of Parliament had their curtains soaked in chloride of lime to try to disguise it. Even then, on 30th June, the smell was so unbearable that members of Parliament venturing into the library were forced to flee holding handkerchiefs to their noses. Benjamin Disraeli, Leader of the House of Commons at the time, vividly described the Thames as "a Stygian pool reeking with ineffable and unbearable horror." Forced at last to act, Parliament swung into action, and engineer Joseph Bazalgette was commissioned to install a huge sewage system that over the course of the next few years removed the source of the problem and greatly improved London's air.

In the previous three decades there had been three major outbreaks of cholera in London, killing thousands of people each time, the most recent of which, only five years before the Great

Stink, had caused the deaths of over 10,000 Londoners. Much of London's drinking water was taken from the Thames, and it had not yet been accepted that drinking this infected water was the cause of the cholera. However, by cleaning up the Thames to remove the stench, the quality of the drinking water also greatly improved and thus, whilst unplanned, by the late 1860s cholera had been banished from London.[322]

We saw earlier that legislation designed to increase safety can sometimes rebound, but behavioural scientist David Halpern has noticed an unintended benefit following the introduction of mandatory wearing of motorcycle helmets. Not only has it resulted in fewer deaths and injuries for bikers, but it has been accompanied by a, sometimes dramatic, fall in thefts of motorbikes. Although one might think that anyone stooping so low as to steal a motorbike would not hesitate to compound their crime by not wearing a helmet, being helmetless does then make one conspicuous and likely to be pulled over by any passing policeman. It seems that potential motorbike thieves found that carrying their own helmet was too much trouble and they became much less inclined to steal motorbikes. After the policy was introduced in 1980 in what was then West Germany, thefts fell by 60%, whilst Texas saw a reduction of 44%, and both Britain and the Netherlands enjoyed a fall in thefts of about a third after introducing helmet laws. The cynical might presume that these ne'er-do-wells would merely thieve elsewhere, but that doesn't seem to have happened. In West Germany, although thefts of pedal cycles and cars did increase, it was very slight compared to the 100,000 reduction in motorbike thefts.[323]

A different unexpected benefit flagged up by David Halpern was a mysterious seven consecutive year fall in UK suicide rates in the 1960s. It transpired that this was not due to people becoming happier because all of a sudden they could play "Twister" or listen to the Beatles, but for a rather more prosaic reason. Up to that time, gas cookers had been fuelled by coal gas, which is high in deadly carbon monoxide, and poisoning yourself by putting your head in the oven and turning the gas on was the preferred method in almost half of suicide cases. However, as suppliers gradually switched to North Sea natural gas, its much lower carbon monoxide content meant that this method of suicide was no longer possible. One might have thought that the would-be suicide would simply turn to other means, but it became clear that, with the easiest method denied them, almost a third of those who would have died either failed in the attempt or overcame their suicidal urges altogether.[324]

In 2016, suicide accounted for almost 45,000 deaths in the US. By any measure, that is a huge number. The preferred method of Americans is to use a gun, with just over half of suicides doing so.[325] As with the gas oven in the UK in the 1960s, it is a means that is readily available to many Americans, as about a third of American households keep at least one gun. As happened when coal gas was withdrawn in the UK, could it be that, if the most obvious means wasn't as easy to obtain, many would-be American suicides would have more time to reconsider their decision or be forced to opt for a means that is not so reliably fatal? Any form of firearm control is clearly a highly contentious matter in America, but what may not be generally realised is that although many Americans use guns to kill other people (about 11,000 in 2016), over two-thirds of gun deaths are of people killing themselves (almost 23,000 in 2016). If fewer guns were around, not only would fewer people kill themselves with guns, but it is extremely likely that there would be fewer suicides overall.

As well as unintended secondary benefits, there are occasions when we accidentally stumble across something that we weren't looking for at all. In 1754 Horace Walpole coined the word "serendipity" to describe such instances, taking it from an old story about the "Three Princes of Serendip"* who "were always making discoveries, by accidents and sagacity, of things which they were not in quest of... "[326] Serendipity has been described as "like looking for the needle inside a haystack and rolling out of it with the farmer's daughter."[327]

Perhaps the classic instance would be the voyage of Christopher Columbus, merrily setting out in 1492 to attempt to find a westward route to the mystical lands of spice in the Far East, only to discover America (well, technically the Caribbean) lying slap bang in the way.

Many centuries later, in the 1940s, one Dr Harry Coover was on a metaphorical voyage of discovery, searching for both an optically clear plastic that would be suitable for gun sights and a heat-resistant transparent material for the canopies of jet planes. Whilst experimenting, he found a material that was completely unsuitable for either of these tasks due to its extraordinary stickiness. So sticky was it that he was reprimanded for ruining two valuable glass lenses by gluing them together. However, extreme stickiness can be very useful under other circumstances, and so Superglue was born. Not only does it repair household objects, but it is so versatile that, in the Vietnam War, it began to be used on the battlefield to seal the wounds of soldiers, keeping them alive whilst they were transferred to hospital.

However, even Superglue wasn't a complete adhesion panacea, and in 1970 a man called Spencer Silver was trying to develop a different sort of strong glue. On his journey of discovery he came up with one that turned out to be almost completely useless at sticking things together. It was so feeble that it wouldn't even hold two pieces of paper together. For 4 years he tried without success to find some sort of practical use for his glue. Then one day, one of his colleagues, Art Fry, who sang in a church choir and had been continually frustrated that his bookmarks kept falling out of his hymnbook, applied some of Spencer's glue to them so that they stayed in place but could be pulled off when required without damaging the page.

Eventually, in 1977, executives at Spencer's company 3M were persuaded that this could have more widespread applications, and so the "Post-it Note" was launched and began its rise to ubiquity. Although there are now many other competing brands, 3M's original version still generates income of over US$1 billion (about £770 million) a year for the company.

Taking advantage of serendipity requires a certain level of curiosity. As we might expect, scientists are particularly well equipped in this regard. So when, in 1903, French chemist Edouard Benedictus accidentally knocked over and broke a glass flask, he didn't automatically sweep the bits up and throw them away. Noticing that, rather than scattering shards to every corner of the lab, the broken pieces stayed together, he investigated further. The flask had been sitting around for a while and the plastic which it had held had evaporated, leaving a thin layer coating the glass. When the glass shattered, it was this coating that had held the bits together. Edouard realised that this would make glass very much safer for people who smashed into it, and countless car drivers have been thankful for his unintendedly invented safety glass.

Another man who discovered the benefit of an apparently empty vessel was the young chemist Dr Roy J. Plunkett. Whereas most of us might merely berate a tank that didn't dispense the gas that we were sure was inside, Dr Plunkett had a curiosity of the highest order. In 1938, whilst working for the DuPont chemical company, he was searching, like Thomas Midgley after him, for a safe refrigerant. He opened a valve on a cylinder which should have been full of the gas Tetrafluoroethylene and was surprised to find that none came out. Having calculated from the weight of the tank that the Tetrafluoroethylene *was* inside, he fiddled about with the valve to make sure that that was working properly. It was then that he took a very impressive step, and went to the trouble of sawing the cylinder open. Inside, he found that the gas had somehow coalesced into a waxy white powder.

Being a scientist, he began to investigate the properties of this mysterious substance, and as he did so he grew increasingly excited. It turned out to be a polymer which was extremely slippery and was not affected by strong acids, heat or solvents. However, producing it would have been very expensive, and no practical commercial use was found for it at that time. It consequently sat on a shelf until midway through the Second World War, when General Leslie R. Groves had a conversation with a DuPont chemist. General Groves was head of the Manhattan Project, developing the atomic bomb, and required a material that would resist the fearsomely corrosive gas Uranium Hexafluoride. It turned out that the new polymer was perfect for the job. Development of the material (now being marketed as "Teflon") continued steadily after the war, leading to the use for which we perhaps best know it today, coating saucepans. It was also discovered that, if inserted into the human body, it is one of the few substances that isn't rejected, and so it is also used in life-saving applications such as artificial heart valves and pacemakers as well as replacement joints, corneas, tracheas, tendons and dentures. Roy J. Plunkett's accidental discovery has even been used on the Moon to insulate cables and is used to shield the nose cones of spaceships from the terrific heat they endure when re-entering the Earth's atmosphere.[328]

Chemists seem to be particularly good at spotting an unintended beneficial consequence. During his Easter break from college in 1856, 18-year-old chemist William Perkin carried out some experiments at home whilst trying to find a synthetic replacement for the malaria drug quinine. One particular experiment produced an unpromising black sludge, but whilst cleaning out the flask with alcohol, he found that the resulting solution turned silk a purple colour which proved impossible to wash out. He had inadvertently discovered the first ever synthetic dye. Until that time, the only way to produce purple dye was to take a secretion from particular sea snails and then expose it to sunlight for just the right amount of time. This was not an efficient process, and as many as a quarter of a million snails could be needed for just one ounce of dye.[329] So, instead of returning to college, William decided to market this new dye, which he called "mauveine" or "mauve", and he achieved enormous success astonishingly quickly. Within 2 years the Empress Eugénie, wife of Napoleon III, was wearing mauve, and when Queen Victoria wore the colour to her daughter Victoria's wedding in 1858 his future was assured.[330]

Medical research seems to be another especially ripe field for inadvertent discoveries. In 1956 inventor Wilson Greatbatch was attempting to build a device to record heart rhythms at the University of Buffalo. During one experiment he accidentally put a resistor of the wrong size into the circuit and was surprised to hear the device producing electrical pulses instead of recording them. However, rather than just replacing the resistor, his curiosity was excited by his realisation that the pulses sounded very much like human heartbeats. He was aware that other scientists were trying to find a way to electrically stimulate the heart in order to rectify breakdowns in the heart's natural rhythm, but that the only existing pacemakers were large external units which ran on mains electricity. He instantly saw that this tiny device could be inserted into patients to stimulate heartbeats. By 1960 the first human patient had been operated on, and by the time of his death in 2011, over half a million pacemakers were being implanted every year, hugely increasing life expectancy and quality of life for many millions of people.[331, 332] Very satisfyingly, pacemakers make use of one of our other unintended discoveries, Teflon.

Heart research led to another spectacular accidental success in the 1990s. Scientists at Pfizer were searching for a drug that would treat high blood pressure and angina. They created a drug called sildenafil citrate, but the early tests were disappointing. Another apparent drawback was that it had a somewhat startling side effect, as men who were taking it found that they were experiencing unexpected erections. The scientists went off down this path instead, and in 1998 a new anti-impotence drug, now marketed as Viagra, was launched, achieving worldwide sales in excess of US$1 billion (about £770 million) within a year.

As a further happy unintended consequence, a number of endangered animal species may be grateful for Viagra's invention. The velvet covering of reindeer antlers and the penises of Canadian hooded and harp seals have long been used in traditional Chinese medicine for their supposedly anti-impotence qualities. However, once Viagra became available, it quickly became apparent that it was easier to obtain, cheaper and rather more effective, and so the demand for reindeer antlers fell by 72% between 1997 and 1998, whilst the demand for seal penises fell by half between 1996 and 1998.[333]

These discoveries all came about when people were already looking for something, but sometimes, curiosity in even the most commonplace of circumstances can yield extraordinary results. Throughout the ages, people have been walking in the countryside, and for almost as long have been coming home to discover that seeds have become attached to their clothing. One particular seed, the cocklebur, is especially difficult to detach, but it was not until 1948 that one man, George de Mestral, became sufficiently curious about its properties. Returning from a walk in the woods, he found that both he and his dog had become covered in burrs, which proved to be a nightmare to disentangle from the dog's fur. Intrigued by their tenacious grip, he inspected some under a microscope, where he saw that they had a beautiful system of hooks, enabling them to attach themselves to passing animals and walkers, and thus spread the plant far and wide. So fascinated was he that he spent the next 10 years developing the fixative that we now know as "Velcro" (the word deriving from "velvet" and "crochet"), which is used wherever a quick, simple fastening and release system is required.[334] Like Teflon, Velcro has been to the Moon, being used to fasten gloves and bags and to attach watches and other items to space suits. The Apollo 17 astronauts even fixed a small piece inside their helmets and used it as a nose scratcher.[335,336] By 2015 the Velcro company had 2,500 employees and estimated worldwide sales of US$500 million (about £380 million).[337]

If an amazing invention such as this can spring from just a walk in the woods, who knows what we ourselves might discover if we keep our minds sufficiently open?

* Serendip is now known as Sri Lanka.

Chapter 9

So – how can we do good better?

We have seen that failing to take unintended consequences into account can have terrible results. Indeed, it's been going on for a long time. Some 3,000 years ago, wise (if somewhat Eeyoreish) King Solomon had discovered that, "There is a way which seems right to a man, but its end is the way of death."[338] Hopefully our unintended consequences won't be quite so dramatic but how can we avoid taking the path that seems right, and yet ends disastrously?

Let's take a look first at our interactions with others.

If we are trying to deal with distressed or suspiciously acting people, as we reflected earlier, commands such as, "Calm down!" or "Come here!" will generally not have the hoped-for result. It might be better to try something along the lines of, "It's going to be all right. Talk to me. What's the matter?" or to walk casually in their direction before asking, "Excuse me, could I chat with you for a moment?" This is the sort of advice that Dr George J. Thompson, president of the previously mentioned Verbal Judo Institute, has given to more than 700,000 American police over the years. They have seen the benefit, and it doesn't just work for the police. Parents may find it all too easy to warn a wayward child that, "I'm not going to tell you again," the effect of which is generally just to add fuel to an already fiery dispute. A better approach might be something like, "Listen, it's important that you understand this, so please pay close attention to what I'm about to tell you." We need to remember that everybody would like to be treated with respect, to be asked rather than told what to do, and would prefer to be offered options instead of just being faced with a threat.[339]

Having made the right initial approach, it's then a good plan to ensure that those involved are informed about the issue. And there is no shortage of information available. In fact, it has been estimated that every day each of us is accosted by enough information to fill at least 150 newspapers. I am writing this paragraph on a train, and as I do so, information is being flung at me from all sides. I read that I am sitting in a Priority Seat, whom I should give it up to if required and the website that I should contact if I require more information. My carriage has the letter F and the number 68427. I am told where the emergency alarm and equipment are situated, and indeed, how to open the doors if there is an emergency. I am directed towards the first aid kit. I am asked to place my hand luggage under the seat. I am warned of the consequences of not having purchased a ticket. I am advised of a website where I can purchase train tickets. I am alerted to the danger of a cupboard door swinging open. I am provided with a map to enable me to plan my journey anywhere in the south-east of England, and with another map showing me the possibilities of further travel within London after my arrival there. On top of all of this potentially useful information, American Express is offering me 5% cashback on certain purchases if I sign up to their credit card (although the huge interest rate seems to deflate the bargain somewhat), whilst Sky is offering me a thrilling package of TV, sports and film entertainment for a (relatively and temporary) bargain price. And on top of all this, a disembodied voice is informing everyone on the train that we will need to be in the front nine coaches if we wish to alight at Riddlesdown station. (Happily, I do not.)

With so much information around, it can be difficult to cut through the fog. It's still all too easy to rely on misconceptions and wrong assumptions. To take one example, the giving of foreign aid can be a contentious subject for voters, and a 2015 study found that over half of Americans felt that their Government was spending too much on it.[340] However, on being further questioned, it transpired that the average respondent believed that a truly massive 26% of government income was being spent on such aid, whereas the actual figure was less than 1%. Once they found out how wrong they were, most changed their minds (although over a quarter still thought that even 1% was too much). Clearly, the right information hadn't been getting through.

As was the case for those voters, it can be all too easy for us to base our actions on incorrect assumptions and thus be blinded to reality. Behavioural economist Dan Ariely discovered this to his cost whilst he was a young man. He had been attending a graduation ceremony, to which somebody had brought along a magnesium shell, intending to add a bit of gusto to the celebrations. However, the shell accidentally exploded whilst Dan was standing nearby, with the result that 70% of his body suffered third-degree burns. During the months that he spent recovering in hospital, his dressings needed changing every day. As he describes the process, "The nurses would rip off the dressings all at once, without a break. It was excruciating, but the nurses insisted that tearing the bandages off was the best way." Dan suggested to them that it might be less painful if they did it more gradually, but they refused, convinced that they were acting in his best interests. Dan, understandably, felt very strongly about the matter, and when he left hospital, he began to conduct his own experiments. These revealed that his suspicion was right and that it was actually preferable to have a longer period of lesser pain rather than short stabs of very intense pain.[341] The strength of their intuition had blinded his nurses to the realisation that they didn't actually have the right information, so that, whilst trying to do the right thing, they were in fact inflicting unnecessary pain on Dan and their other patients.

Making the right sort of information available isn't always enough to change minds though – it also needs to be given in the right way. Overwhelming people with gloomy news can be counterproductive, and climate change researcher Dr Victoria Herrmann has emphasised that, because the stories that we tell help to shape the way in which we make sense of the world, it is vital that we don't present humanity as a hopeless victim. Presented with a disastrous scenario, we actually become *less* likely to try to do something about it. We would do much better to portray people as potential heroes, inspiring them to feel like Luke Skywalker and the Rebel Alliance taking on the Galactic Empire or Harry Potter battling Lord Voldemort. Thus, news about climate change should be leavened with some good news. We might point out that in 2015, 45 times as much solar power was installed worldwide compared to 10 years earlier,[342] that at one time in 2017, 85% of Germany's electricity came from renewable sources,[343] and that in the 10 years to 2017, US CO_2 emissions from energy production fell by 14%.[344] Dr Herrmann found many examples of people taking positive action, such as that of Andra Samoa, who is working in American Samoa to restore mangroves and thus improve the ecosystem and stop the shoreline eroding. Giving real-life examples involves the listener in the story, both harnessing the power of what psychologists call "narrative persuasion" and emphasising possible solutions, so that readers feel empowered to follow suit, rather than just throwing their hands up in despair.[345] This is not a new technique. The British Government, faced with horrendous odds in 1940, went to great lengths to successfully promote a powerfully heroic narrative around the defence of Britain by the Royal Air Force against Nazi Germany. They stressed the solution rather than fixating on the problem. The Earth Optimism movement came into being in 2007 with the intention of bringing this positive element to the debate about conservation and the environment, and flags up the good news stories that so often the media seem to ignore. They tell stories of hope, such as that of our friend the red-cockaded woodpecker and the restoration of Rhode Island's Pawcatuck River, where fish are now able to migrate along the full length of the river for the first time in 250 years. As Professors Andrew Balmford and Nancy Knowlton pointed out in support of the campaign, Martin Luther King, Jr. did not say, "I have a problem," but inspired his listeners with his dream.[346]

And once inspired, it is easy to take the first steps towards improving matters. To give one apparently trivial example, the Minnesota Pollution Control Agency has pointed out that about 40% of the 5 million cars on the state's roads have underinflated tyres, resulting in an extra 300,000 tons of CO_2 being poured into the atmosphere every year.[347] If the tiny action needed to correct that was taken, it would be the equivalent of taking about 65,000 cars off the road. It isn't difficult to believe that car drivers around the world are no more diligent than in Minnesota, so if everybody just took the trouble to do a monthly tyre check, we'd all be helping the world out and saving money at the same time.*

Changing our minds, even in the face of evidence, can be a challenge, but we would do well to remember the saying usually attributed to the economist John Maynard Keynes who, when accused of making a U-turn, apparently responded, "When I find new information, I change my mind. What do you do?"

We have seen how governments, with enormous power at their disposal, have a particular ability to bring about unintended consequences. Prohibition, introduced with the intention of improving the lives of American citizens, enabled the rise of organised crime and led to an increase in murder rates and general criminality. The Patriot Act, intended to make the American banking system more secure and people safer, led to the 2008 crash, bringing years of misery and hardship to hundreds of millions around the world. One way of avoiding disasters such as these could be to take a more subtle approach to a problem. This possibility has now been recognised at the top level of government, and in 2010, the then UK Prime Minister David Cameron established a small department called the Behavioural Insights Team (BIT), giving it a mandate to find more effective ways of communicating with people. One thing that all governments are extremely interested in is maximising tax revenue, but getting some people to pay their taxes can be a difficult, time-consuming and costly operation. BIT experimented by sending different types of letters to the reluctant payers, and discovered that the most successful letters weren't those that threatened dire consequences for not paying, but rather those that played on the recipient's feeling of social responsibility. Just by letting people know that most of their neighbours had already paid their taxes, it was estimated that in a year an extra £30 million (about US$39 million) of tax revenue had been painlessly and cost-effectively collected.

The power of encouragement was illustrated by another experiment, in which people attending adult numeracy and literacy classes were sent inspiring text messages every week. Their attendance improved over the year by 21% and the number passing every exam was 12% better amongst those who had received the encouraging texts.[348]

BIT was given two years in which to save the UK Government £5 million (about US$6.5 million). In fact, it managed to achieve twice that figure, and in 2014 it was partly spun off into the private sector in order to carry on its work more widely. It has since established projects in many parts of the world, including the US, Australia, Poland, Mexico and Costa Rica, and it is also working with the World Bank and the UN.

Normalising tax payment, as the BIT notices did, has worked very successfully, but sadly, normalising the *wrong* type of behaviour can be equally effective at encouraging behaviour that you want to avoid. The Petrified Forest National Park in Arizona, famed for its fossilised wood, was faced with the problem that tourists, keen to take home a memento of their visit, were steadily dismantling the very attraction that they had come to see. So the National Park Service erected signs pointing out that, "Your heritage is being vandalized every day by theft losses of petrified wood of 14 tons a year, mostly a small piece at a time." However, what the authorities had unwittingly done was to point out that, "Everyone does it," thus making the act socially acceptable. As a result, thefts of wood actually tripled after the notices were put up.[349]

Following this example, many sites of geographical significance around the world, including Australia's Great Barrier Reef, have adopted a rather different approach. The mantra, "Take nothing but photos, leave nothing but footprints," is stressed, making it clear that the normal course of action is to resist temptation. A few years ago I visited an island on the Barrier Reef, and as far as I was aware this maxim was adhered to by every one of my fellow tourists – with not a single pebble or shell being taken. And knowing that I could just enjoy the experience without agonising about which souvenir to take proved to be very relaxing.

There are other instances where we might take the opportunity to encourage rather than scold. Megan Smith, one-time chief technology officer to President Obama, feels that a better way of promoting gender diversity in the tech world is not to attack the tech companies for their failure in this respect, but to flag up how many great female technologists there have been. One of the approaches that she took was to push Google to celebrate female mathematicians and scientists in the occasional "Doodles" that first appeared on its homepage in 1998. Shockingly, in the first seven years of the Doodles being used, not one female historical figure had been celebrated, but by 2013, women accounted for 22% of people-related international Doodles.[350] By normalising the role of women in this field, hopefully more girls will feel encouraged to steer themselves towards it as a possible career, increasing the number of female applicants and making it easier for tech companies to employ them in the future.[351]

Another way in which governments can avoid having their actions backfire is to take a more experimental approach to legislation. In the business world, companies naturally spring up and disappear all the time, but governments, wary perhaps of being accused of U-turning, tend to plough ahead with their policies no matter how ill-advised they might be. Margaret Thatcher's Government was a case in point. Having introduced the hugely unpopular Poll Tax in England in 1990, it took rioting on the streets of London to convince the Government that it had made a mistake and it was forced to replace it with a fairer system. Gradually rolling out new legislation (and – vitally – listening properly to the feedback) would enable teething problems to be more easily resolved. Another way of ensuring that legislation is doing its job properly is to make it subject to a "sunset provision", so that, unless people see that it is working and renew it, it automatically expires at a certain time.

Whatever we do, it's wise to consider the wider implications of our actions. If the genius at HMRC who rerouted all the post via a central hub had only taken a moment to consider how the ensuing delays might throw an almighty spanner in an already creaking system, they would surely have reconsidered.

HMRC was being pressurised to save money. They tried to do that by taking action. And when faced with an issue, it is perhaps the hardest thing in the world to resist trying to actively do something about it. But sometimes the best course is to resist that impulse. As the philosopher Blaise Pascal sadly mused, "All of humanity's problems stem from man's inability to sit quietly in a room alone."[352] The wise medic knows that this may well be the best policy when it comes to our health. As US doctor Garrison Bliss has stated, "Doing nothing trumps doing something most of the time. Or as I heard during my internship – 'Don't just do something, stand there!'"[353] Not only might this be better for the patient, but a study by a group of academics in

October 2011 calculated that by not carrying out a number of pointless procedures, US doctors could save almost US$7 billion (over £5 billion) a year.[354] There is nothing new in this, for as Hippocrates, the father of Medicine, put it over 2,000 years ago, "To do nothing is sometimes a good remedy." It is a remedy that still works today.

Extraordinarily, there have been times when doing nothing at all has resulted in fewer people dying. In January 1976, 50% of doctors in Los Angeles County, California, went on strike and refused to carry out any but emergency procedures. One might have worried for the populace, but the bizarre result was that over the next seven weeks the death rate declined from an initial 21 per 100,000 of the population to just 14 – a five-year low. Indeed, a study of five different occasions when doctors in various parts of the world went on strike revealed that during each of those times, the local death rate either remained the same or actually fell.[355] This counter-intuitive statistic illustrates that, when Dr Bliss' preferred "doing nothing" strategy is the default position, it has turned out to be safer than unnecessary interference.**

We can also see the benefits of "doing nothing" in other walks of life. The world's best known (and arguably most successful) investor, Warren Buffett, is a man who has made inactivity his axiom. As he said in his 1990 letter to his shareholders:

Lethargy bordering on sloth remains the cornerstone of our investment style: This year we neither bought nor sold a share of five of our six major holdings.

By May 2017, his investment fund, Berkshire Hathaway, held over US$400 billion (over £300 billion) in assets, whilst the value of a single share in the fund rose over a thousand-fold between 1980 and 2017. And, Terry Smith, another fund manager, whose UK Fundsmith fund has actually outperformed Warren Buffett's since its 2010 launch, pithily summarises his own strategy as, "Buy good companies. Don't overpay. Do nothing."[356]

Hopefully, you now feel equipped and ready to do battle against the foe of unintended consequences. Thinking before reacting, making sure you have the right information, not making assumptions, being ready to nudge rather than cajole, keen to emphasise the good rather than the bad, ready to experiment and quite prepared to do nothing when the need arises.

But however hard we try to avoid unintended consequences, it's worth recognising that sometimes we may just have to accept that they are a necessary but worthwhile price to pay. As UK MP Andrew Mitchell has written about foreign aid, "If we want to give our aid to places where it will be spent without any worries about unintended consequences or the risk of corruption, we might as well give it to Sweden or Switzerland. But the point, and the paradox, is that the people most in need of our aid are, by definition, the people who are hardest to help... We should be generous and open-hearted – but match this compassion with a laser-like focus on outcomes."[357]

As we've seen, people who are curious seem to be well-placed to take advantage of unexpected benefits. We can apply this to our lives in simple ways and sometimes it can be worthwhile trying new things just to see if an unexpected benefit might result. So, instead of waiting for a transport strike, why not try a different route for your regular journey every now and then? Or strike up a conversation with someone you've never spoken to before. Or randomly visit somewhere new. You could try saying yes to more things or learning a new skill. Give it a go and you might just find yourself alighting in the land of Serendip.

---

* Stirred into action myself on reading this, I was embarrassed to find that my own car's tyres were underinflated, and have taken remedial action.

** Of course, this is not to suggest for a moment that one should not consult a doctor about any troubling symptoms. A doctor deciding to do nothing and us deciding to do nothing are entirely different matters...

References

1. Wallace-Wells, Ben (2007) "How America Lost the War on Drugs", *Rolling Stone*, 13th December

2. (2003) Interview with *Rolling Stone*, December 2003

3. "Hurricane Neddy" (1996) *The Simpsons*, Season 8, Episode 8

4. Kuhrt, Jon (2011) "When helping doesn't help", *Third Way*, p. 24, May

5. http://www.streetlink.org.uk/

6. *Metro* (2014) p. 14, 6th May

7. Thompson, Dr George (2005) "7 things never to say to anyone, and why". Available at: http://policeone.com/communications/articles/120708

8. Lott, Tim (2015) "Bedtimes are really stressful and my solution is to simply give up", *The Guardian*, 21st February

9. Worley, Will (2017) *The Independent*, 27th June

10. (2007) "How severe is subprime mess?", *Associated Press*. Available at: www.msnbc.msn.com/id/17584725, 13th March

11. First American CoreLogic study, cited in Arnold, Chris (2007) "Economists Brace for Worsening Subprime Crisis", 7th August. Available at: www.npr.org/templates/story/story.php?storyId=12561184

12. McDonald, Lawrence (2010) "The Lehman Brothers Hangover", *Daily Beast*, 15th September

13. Pittman, Mark and Ivry, Bob (2009) "U.S. Taxpayers Risk $9.7 Trillion on Bailout Programs", www.Bloomberg.com, 9th February. Available at: http://www.informationclearinghouse.info/article22581.htm

14. National Fraud Authority Report (2011) "Procurement Fraud in the Public Sector", p. 16, October

15. Radnedge, Aidan (2011) "Online conmen take millions off

councils", *Metro*, 10th November

16. Curtis, Polly (2010) *The Guardian*, 19th November

17. Oates, Wallace and Schwab, Robert (2013) "The Window Tax: A Case In Excess Burden", *Journal of Economic Perspectives*, October

18. Lewis, Paul (2015) "Can't Pay, Won't Pay", BBC R4 *MoneyBox*, 18th May

19. https://democracy.maldon.gov.uk/documents/s5276/ Appendix%201.pdf

20. Guthrie, Thomas (1867) "How to Get Rid of an Enemy", *The Sunday Magazine*. Cited in Oates, Wallace and Schwab, Robert (2013) "The Window Tax – A Case In Excess Burden", *Journal of Economic Perspectives*, October

21. (2012) *Sunday Times*, 29th January

22. Harford, Tim (2006) *The Undercover Economist*, Little, Brown, pp. 96–97

23. Genesis 47:24

24. Quoted in Adam Smith Institute briefing paper (Undated), "Estimated revenue losses from Capital Gains Tax increases". Available at: www.hmrc.gov.uk/stats/capital_gains/table14-1.pdf

25. Sommerlad, Nick (2011) *Daily Mirror*, 19th January

26. Harford, Tim (2011) "Taxing my music can't be good, can it?", *Financial Times*, 9th November

27. Gans, Joshua and Leigh, Andrew (2006) "Did the Death of Australian Inheritance Taxes Affect Deaths?" *Topics in Economic Analysis & Policy*: Vol. 6:Iss 1, Article 23

28. Gans, Joshua and Leigh, Andrew (2008) "Born on the first of July: An (un)natural experiment in birth timing", *Journal of Public Economics* 93, pp. 246–263, 24th July

29. Colella, Anton (2015) "Our bulging tax code is holding Britain back: Politicians must fix this", *City A.M.*, 25th March

30. Warner, Jeremy (2012) "The UK tax system is at breaking

point", *Daily Telegraph*, 1ˢᵗ March

31. Taylor, Joel (2010) *Metro*, 5ᵗʰ May

32. Guest, Greta (2014) "How companies can minimize the stigma of affirmative action", *University of Michigan News*, 12ᵗʰ August. The study referred to is (2014) "The Stigma of Affirmative Action: A Stereotyping-Based Theory and Meta-Analytic Test of the Consequences for Performance", *Academy of Management Journal*, August

33. Sherwin, Adam (2015) "Peter Alliss: Equality for women has 'b******d up' golf", *The Independent*, 7ᵗʰ April

34. Leith, Sam (2010) *London Evening Standard*, 1ˢᵗ March

35. Pickard, Jim and Stacey, Kiran (2015) "Freedom of information is Mission Impossible for Downing St emails", *Financial Times*, June 16. Available from: http://on.ft.com/1QCbS8a

36. Gopnik, Adam (2015) "A Point of View: The guilty thrill of reading other people's mail", BBC Radio 4, 17ᵗʰ July

37. (2005) "How we made the Millennium Dome", Richard Rogers interviewed by Oliver Wainwright, *The Guardian*, 17ᵗʰ March

38. (2000) "The Millennium Dome", National Audit Office Report, pp. 39–41, 9ᵗʰ November

39. (2000) "The Millennium Dome", National Audit Office Report, p. 13, 9ᵗʰ November

40. (2005) "The regeneration of the Millennium Dome and associated land", House of Commons Committee of Public Accounts report, 18ᵗʰ July

41. Braund, Mark (2007) *The Guardian*, 22ⁿᵈ June

42. *Eye: The story behind the London Eye* (2007) Marks Barfield Architects, London: Black Dog Publishing

43. Case Study 013, "The Eden Project". Available at: http://www.communityplanning.net/casestudies/pdfs/013/Casestudy013.pdf

44. (2007) *The Guardian*, quoting from Tim Smit's speech to the

Social Enterprise Coalition Voice 07, 31st January

45. Ajemian, Robert (1987) "Where is the real George Bush?" *Time*, 26th January

46. Proverbs 29:18

47. (2001) "Showbiz meets science", *The Economist*, 16th August

48. (2001) "Showbiz meets science", *The Economist*, 16th August

49. (2010) BPI "Digital Music Nation" Report

50. (2011) British games publishing trade organisation UKIE report

51. Butcher, Mike (2010) "The Digital Economy Bill: a nightmare of unintended consequences", *Daily Telegraph* blog, 8th April

52. Smith, Richard (2010) *Daily Mirror*, 25th November; and Wilkes, David (2010) *Daily Mail*, 25th November

53. Dubner, Stephen J. and Levitt, Steven D. (2008) "The Case Of The Red-Cockaded Woodpecker", *New York Times Magazine*, 20th January

54. Peltzman, Sam (2004) "Regulation and the Natural Progress of Opulence", AEI-Brookings, Joint Center 2004 Distinguished Lecture, 8th September

55. (2011) *Metro*, 12th October

56. Harford, Tim (2014) "When regulators are all out to déjeuner", *Financial Times*, 26th September

57. (2012) *Today* programme, BBC Radio 4, 31st May

58. Simpson, Jack (2014) "Plymouth University to take down anti-cheating posters after they were found to be helping students cheat", *The Independent*, 4th May

59. Coleridge, ST (1836) *Letters, Conversations, and Recollections of S. T. Coleridge: Volume 2*

60. (2001) "Nicotine", *Encyclopedia of Drugs, Alcohol and Addictive Behavior*, Gale Cengage

61. (2004) "Calling time: the nation's drinking as a major health issue", Academy of Medical Sciences, London AMS

62. Sacks, Dr Jeffrey J., Brewer et al (2015) "2010 National and

State Costs of Excessive Alcohol Consumption", *American Journal of Preventive Medicine*, 1st October

63. Langford, Andrew (2012) "British Liver Trust", *Metro*, 22nd March

64. www.ias.org.uk/Alcohol-knowledge-centre/Economic-impacts/Factsheets/Economic-costs.aspx

65. Sacks, Dr Jeffrey J., Brewer et al (2015) "2010 National and State Costs of Excessive Alcohol Consumption", *American Journal of Preventive Medicine*, 1st October

66. Asbury, Herbert (1950) *The Great Illusion: An Informal History of Prohibition*, New York: Doubleday, quoted in Behr, Edward (1998) *Prohibition: Thirteen Years That Changed America*, Penguin Books/BBC Books

67. Behr, Edward (1998) *Prohibition: Thirteen Years That Changed America*, Penguin Books/BBC Books, p. 17

68. (1920) *Anti-Saloon League of America Yearbook*, Anti-Saloon League of America, American Issue Press, p. 28

69. Sinclair, Andrew (1962) *Prohibition: The Era of Excess*, Little, Brown, p. 198

70. (2008) "Teaching With Documents: The Volstead Act and Related Prohibition Documents", United States National Archives, 14th February

71. Lee, Henry (1963) *How Dry We Were: Prohibition Revisited*, Englewood Cliffs: Prentice Hall Inc., p. 68

72. Lerner, Michael, "Unintended Consequences" in *Prohibition*. Available at: www.pbs.org

73. Behr, Edward (1998) *Prohibition: Thirteen Years That Changed America*, Penguin Books/BBC Books, p. 195

74. Miron, Jeffrey (2001) "Alcohol Prohibition", EH.net Encyclopedia, 24th September. Available at: http://eh.net/encyclopedia/alcohol-prohibition/

75. (2016) "Debate fact-check: Hillary Clinton and Donald Trump's claims reviewed", *The Guardian*, 10th October

76. Woodiwiss, Michael (2005) *Gangster Capitalism: The United*

States and The Global Rise of Organized Crime, Constable and Robinson Ltd., p. 51

77. Lerner, Michael, "Unintended Consequences" in *Prohibition*. Available at: www.pbs.org

78. Blum, Deborah (2010) "The little-told story of how the U.S. government poisoned alcohol during Prohibition with deadly consequences". Available at: www.slate.com, 19th February

79. Behr, Edward (1998) *Prohibition: Thirteen Years That Changed America*, Penguin Books/BBC Books, p. 219

80. Davis, Marni (2012) *Jews and Booze: Becoming American in the Age of Prohibition*, New York University Press, p. 145

81. (1928) "Statistical Abstract of the United States: 1928", Washington DC: US Bureau of the Census, p. 767, quoted in Blocker, Jr., PhD, Jack S. (2006) "Did Prohibition Really Work? Alcohol Prohibition as a Public Health Innovation", *American Journal of Public Health*, pp. 233–243

82. Behr, Edward (1998) *Prohibition: Thirteen Years That Changed America*, Penguin Books/BBC Books, p. 95

83. Behr, Edward (1998) *Prohibition: Thirteen Years That Changed America*, Penguin Books/BBC Books, pp. 106–108

84. Behr, Edward (1998) *Prohibition: Thirteen Years That Changed America*, Penguin Books/BBC Books, p. 102

85. Dickson, Paul (2015) *Contraband Cocktails: How America Drank When It Wasn't Supposed To*, Melville House, p. 42

86. National Commission on Marihuana and Drug Abuse (n.d.) "History of Alcohol Prohibition"

87. Mencken, HL (1980) *A Choice of Days*, New York: Knopf

88. Behr, Edward (1998) *Prohibition: Thirteen Years That Changed America*, Penguin Books/BBC Books, p. 92

89. Cowen, Tyler (2011) speaking in "How American food got so bad", Freakonomics Radio podcast, 14th December. Available at: http://freakonomics.com/2011/12/14/how-american-food-got-so-bad-full-transcript/

90. Behr, Edward (1998) *Prohibition: Thirteen Years That Changed America*, Penguin Books/BBC Books, p. 94

91. Ade, George (1931) *The Old-Time Saloon*, New York: Ray Long and Richard R. Smith, p. 51

92. Hough, Andrew et al (2011) *Daily Telegraph*, 14th July

93. (2012) *This Is Lincolnshire*, 25th May

94. "Deadly fake vodka gang jailed" (2013) HMRC Press Release, 25th January. Available at: www.mynewsdesk.com

95. Ford, Richard (2015) "Violent crime drops by a third after rise in alcohol prices", *The Times*, 22nd April

96. (2011) "The battle of the bottle", *The Economist*, 3rd December

97. (2017) "New scheme to help reduce City street crime has launched", City of London Police, 20th July. Available at: http://news.cityoflondon.police.uk/r/863/new_scheme_to_help_reduce_city_street_crime_has_l

98. (2010) "Partnership – Kingston Street Pastors", *London Evening Standard*, 25th October

99. Quoted in Mason, Rowena (2008) "Street pastors making a difference after-hours", *Daily Telegraph*, 1st June

100. Peters, Gretchen (2009) "How Opium Profits the Taliban", United States Institute of Peace (Peaceworks no. 62.), p. 23

101. Costa, A. (2008) "Making drug control 'fit for purpose': Building on the UNGASS decade", UN Office on Drugs and Crime

102. Hughes, Chris (2012) *Daily Mirror*, 13th July

103. Quoted in Wallace-Wells, Ben (2007) "How America Lost the War on Drugs", *Rolling Stone*, 13th December

104. Payan, Tony, political scientist at the University of Texas-El Paso, quoted in Wallace-Wells, Ben (2007) "How America Lost the War on Drugs", *Rolling Stone*, 13th December

105. Miglierini, Julian (2011) *BBC News*, 14th January

106. Axworthy, Jon (2012) *Shortlist*, 15th March

107. US Government figures quoted in Green, Graeme (2014) "Toking gesture or a dope idea?", *Metro*, 20th January

108. Aitkenhead, Decca (2016) "I have done really bad things", the Saturday interview, *The Guardian*, 27th August

109. Rifkind, Hugo (2012) "For a genius drugs policy, look to California", *The Times*, 16th October

110. Burns, Ed et al (2008) *Time* magazine, 5th March

111. (2014) "Prisoners in 2013", Washington DC: US Department of Justice, Bureau of Justice Statistics, September, NCJ 1247282, p. 16

112. (2012) "A Fresh Approach To Drugs", UK Drug Policy Commission, October, p. 9

113. Couvée, Koos (2016) "There's one real way to stop gang crime: legalise drugs", *The Spectator*, 13th February

114. (2012) "A Fresh Approach To Drugs", UK Drug Policy Commission, October, pp. 13–14

115. Cole, Claire et al (2010) "A Guide to Adulterants, Bulking Agents and Other Contaminants Found in Illicit Drugs", Centre For Public Health, April

116. Bhattacharjee, Yudhijit (2012) *Wired* magazine, 19th July

117. (n.d.) Castillo, Mariano, "Obama open to new approaches in drug war, but not legalization", CNN. Available at: https://edition.cnn.com/2012/04/14/politics/summit-of-the-americas/index.html

118. Quoted in Green, Graeme (2014) "Toking gesture or a dope idea?", *Metro*, 20th January

119. (2012) "A Fresh Approach To Drugs", UK Drug Policy Commission, October, p. 6

120. Figures quoted in Green, Graeme (2014) "Toking gesture or a dope idea?", *Metro*, 20th January

121. Washtell, Francesca (2016) "Legalising cannabis would raise £1bn in tax say Liberal Democrats", *City A.M.*, 9th March

122. Miller, Joshua (2016) "In Colo., a look at life after marijuana legislation", *Boston Globe*, 22nd February

123. (2016) *In Business*, "Colorado's Big Marijuana Experiment",

BBC Radio 4, 1ˢᵗ May

124. Hooton, Christopher (2015) "A year after marijuana legalisation in Colorado, 'everything's fine' confirm police", *The Independent*, 20ᵗʰ January

125. Miller, Joshua (2016) "In Colo., a look at life after marijuana legislation", *Boston Globe*, 22ⁿᵈ February

126. Hughes, C. and Stevens, A. (n.d) "What can we learn from the Portuguese decriminalisation of illicit drugs?" *BrJ Criminology* (forthcoming). Quoted in Rolles, S. (2010) "An alternative to the war on drugs", *BMJ* 2010;340:c3360

127. Degenhardt, L. et al (2008) "Toward a Global View of Alcohol, Tobacco, Cannabis, and Cocaine Use: Findings from the WHO World Mental Health Surveys", *PloS Med* 5(7): e141. Quoted in Rolles, S. (2010) "An alternative to the war on drugs", *BMJ* 2010;340:c3360

128. Grillo, Ioan (2015) "US Legalization of Marijuana Has Hit Mexican Cartels' Cross-Border Trade", *Time*, 8ᵗʰ April

129. (2014) "Ending the Drug Wars: Report of the LSE Expert Group on the Economics of Drug Policy"

130. Quoted in Metaal, Pien (2016) "To win the war on drugs, stop brutalising farmers who grow them", *The Guardian*, 19ᵗʰ April

131. Webb, Sam (2014) "Not Afghanistan, but Hampshire! How opium poppies are being grown in the UK to make morphine for the NHS", *Daily Mail*, 24ᵗʰ June

132. (2014) "Ending the Drug Wars: Report of the LSE Expert Group on the Economics of Drug Policy"

133. Grillo, Ioan (2015) "US Legalization of Marijuana Has Hit Mexican Cartels' Cross-Border Trade", *Time*, 8ᵗʰ April

134. Housley, Adam (2015) "More meth, heroin smuggled at US-Mexico border because of laxer marijuana laws, feds say", Fox News Latino, 19ᵗʰ May. Available at: https://www.foxnews.com/world/more-meth-heroin-smuggled-at-u-s-mexico-border-because-of-laxer-marijuana-laws-

feds-say

135. (2014) "Ending the Drug Wars: Report of the LSE Expert Group on the Economics of Drug Policy"

136. Aitkenhead, Decca (2016) "I have done really bad things", the Saturday interview, *The Guardian*, 27th August

137. Burkeman, Oliver (2013) "From weight loss to fundraising, 'ironic effects' can sabotage our best-laid plans", Oliver Burkeman's Blog, *The Guardian*, 12th December

138. Cialdini, Robert B. (1984/1993) *Influence: The Psychology of Persuasion*, William Morrow and Company, pp. 248–249

139. Dahl, Melissa (2015) "Why lonely people stay lonely", Science of Us, 19th July. Available at: https://www.huf fingtonpost.com/science-of-us/why-lonely-people-stay-lo_b_7849692.html. Referencing Brooks, Alison Wood (2014) Harvard Business School. Available at: http://nymag.com/scienceofus/2014/06/how-to-get-over-stage-fright-jenny-slate-style.html

140. Wegner, Daniel M. (2009) "How to Think, Say or Do Precisely the Worst Thing for Any Occasion", *Science*, Vol. 325, 23rd July, p. 48

141. (1996) "Norman's collapse paves way for Faldo", *Sports Illustrated*, 22nd April

142. Syed, Matthew (2010) *Bounce: The Myth of Talent and the Power of Practice*, Fourth Estate, p. 169

143. Syed, Matthew (2010) *Bounce: The Myth of Talent and the Power of Practice*, Fourth Estate, p. 170

144. (2014) *The Apprentice*, Series 10, Episode 10, BBC

145. Fitzsimons, Declan (2016) "Childless at 52: How sweet it would be to be called Dad", *The Guardian*, 13th August

146. Syed, Matthew (2010) *Bounce: The Myth of Talent and the Power of Practice*, Fourth Estate, p. 171

147. Syed, Matthew (2010) *Bounce: The Myth of Talent and the Power of Practice*, Fourth Estate, p. 177

148. Tappin, Neil (2015) "How to cure the putting yips", *Golf*

Monthly, 4th November. Available at: www.golf-monthly.
co.uk/tips/putting/how-to-cure-the-putting-yips-83211

149. Busch, Bradley (2017) "What is the psychological state underlying 'clutch performance' – excelling under pressure?", *The British Psychological Society Research Digest*, 29th June. Available at: https://digest.bps.org.uk/2017/06/29/what-is-the-psychological-state-underlying-clutch-performance-excelling-under-pressure/

150. www.trekkiedating.com, www.trekpassions.com, www.trekdating.com and www.startrekdating.com

151. Orr, Deborah (2015) "Why does choice narrow our tastes, not broaden them?", *The Guardian*, 14th March

152. Kay, John (2010) "Choice", *Financial Times*, 1st October

153. Iyengar, Sheena S. and Lepper, Mark R. (2000) "When Choice is Demotivating: Can One Desire Too Much of a Good Thing?", 19th June. Referenced in Karlan, Dean and Appel, Jacob (2011) *More Than Good Intentions*, Penguin Group, p. 47

154. (2014) "The downside of too many product choices on store shelves", January. Available at: www.consumerreports.org/cro/magazine/2014/too-many-product-choices-in-supermarkets/index.htm

155. Wood, Zoe and Butler, Sarah (2015) "Tesco cuts range by 30% to simplify shopping", *The Guardian*, 30th January

156. Ariely, Dan (Professor of Behavioral Economics, Duke University) and Elbel, Brian (Assistant Professor of Medicine and Health Policy, NYU) in conversation (2008) "Too Many Health Care Choices", Arming The Donkeys podcast. Available at: https://radiopublic.com/arming-the-donkeys-Wk2XPq/ep/s1!6dad7

157. Finkel, Eli et al (2012) "Online Dating: A Critical Analysis from the Perspective of Psychological Science", *Psychological Science in the Public Interest*, 2nd February

158. (2012) "The modern matchmakers", *The Economist*, 11th

February

159. Ormerod, Paul (2016) "How technology is increasing inequality – and it's nothing to do with artificial intelligence", *City A.M.*, 23rd March

160. Quoted in Konnikova, Maria (2013) "A List of Reasons Why Our Brains Love Lists", *New Yorker Online*, 2nd December. Available at: https://www.newyorker.com/tech/annals-of-technology/a-list-of-reasons-why-our-brains-love-lists

161. Henry, Diana (2015) "Help! There's too much choice in the supermarket (and it's all mediocre anyway)", *Daily Telegraph*, 21st October

162. McEwen, Ben (2013) in presentation at Music Publishers' Association, 11th March

163. (2013) "Energy Bill: Committee Stage Report" research paper 13/19, 12 March

164. Brignall, Miles (2012) "Energy bills: the hidden shock", *The Guardian*, 29th June

165. (2013) "CMU Beef of the Week #144: Beyoncé v Buzzfeed", 8th February. Available at: http://www.completemusicupdate.com/article/cmu-beef-of-the-week-144-beyonce-v-buzzfeed/

166. Doughty, Steve (2011) *Daily Mail*, 24th May

167. Le Marie, Nicole (2014) "All I wanted was a hairdo but what I got was a set-to", *Metro*, 9th April

168. Syed, Matthew (2015) "How to blame less and learn more", *The Guardian*, 3rd October

169. Ariely, Dan et al (2009) "Large Stakes and Big Mistakes", *Review of Economic Studies* 76, pp. 451–469

170. Kohn, Alfie (1993) "Why Incentive Plans Cannot Work", *Harvard Business Review*, September-October

171. Grant, Adam and Singh, Jitendra (2011) "The Problem with Financial Incentives – and What to Do About It", Wharton School, University of Pennsylvania, 30th March. Available at: http://knowledge.wharton.upenn.edu/article/the-probl

em-with-financial-incentives-and-what-to-do-about-it/

172. (2009) "The Turner Review: A regulatory response to the global banking crisis", Financial Services Authority, March

173. Harford, Tim (2016) "Why central bankers shouldn't have skin in the game", *Financial Times*, 21st September

174. Jenkins, Simon (2012) "With a ban on bonuses, Fred Goodwin could even have kept his knighthood", *The Guardian*, 31st January

175. (2016) "Neil Woodford scraps bonus pay at his investment firm", *BBC News*, 23rd August. Available at: http://www.bbc.co.uk/news/business-37161654

176. Richins, Marsha L. and Chaplin, Lan Nguyen (2015) "Material Parenting: How the Use of Goods in Parenting Fosters Materialism in the Next Generation", *Journal of Consumer Research*, Vol. 41, April, DOI: 10.1086/680087

177. Twain, Mark (1876) *Tom Sawyer*, Chapter 2

178. Twain, Mark (1876) *Tom Sawyer*, Chapter 2

179. 2 Samuel 10:1–6

180. Portillo, Michael (2013) *1913 – The Year Before*, Episode 10, BBC Radio 4, 21st June

181. Beaumont, Peter (2002) *The Observer*, 8th September

182. Maktab al-Khidamat, also known as Al-Kifah

183. Weaver, Mary Anne (2000) "The Real Bin Laden", *New Yorker*, 24th January

184. Weaver, Mary Anne (1996) "Blowback", *The Atlantic Online*, May

185. (1994) *Boston Herald*, 24th January

186. Filkins, Dexter (2015) "Did George W. Bush create ISIS?", *New Yorker*, 15th May

187. Kaufman, Ted (2015) "Even Putin faces ire of unintended consequences", 3rd July. Available at: https://eu.delawareonline.com/story/opinion/columnists/carron-phillips/2015/07/03/even-putin-faces-ire-unintended-consequences/29637049/

188. Barack Obama interviewed on *Vice News*, quoted in Saul, Heather (2015) "President Obama claims rise of Isis is 'unintended consequence' of George W. Bush's invasion in Iraq", *The Independent*, 18th March

189. Napoleoni, Loretta (2010) *Terrorism and the Economy: How the War on Terror is Bankrupting the World*, Chapter 10, "The Politics of Fear", Seven Stories Press

190. Quoted in (2011) "Is an end in sight?", *Metro*, 14th September

191. Hulsman, John and Palay, Lara (2014) "The West's critical analytical flaw that spawned 80 years of Mid East failure", *City A.M.*, 26th August

192. Hulsman, John and Palay, Lara (2014) "The West's critical analytical flaw that spawned 80 years of Mid East failure", *City A.M.*, 26th August

193. (c500–750BCE) Tzu, Sun, *The Art of War*, 3.2

194. Crawford, Neta C. (2015) "War-related Death, Injury, and Displacement in Afghanistan and Pakistan 2001–2014", Brown University, 22nd May. Available at: https://watson. brown.edu/costsofwar/files/cow/imce/papers/2015/ War%20Related%20Casualties%20Afghanistan%20 and%20Pakistan%202001-2014%20FIN.pdf

195. Amadeo, Kimberly (2019) "Afghanistan War Cost, Timeline and Economic Impact", The Balance, 2nd January. Available at: https://www.thebalance.com/cost-of-afghanistan-war-timeline-economic-impact-4122493

196. Quoted in Ramo, Joshua Cooper (2009) *The Age of the Unthinkable*, Little, Brown, p. 141

197. Quoted in Ramo, Joshua Cooper (2009) *The Age of the Unthinkable*, Little, Brown, p. 189

198. Cortright, David and Lopez, George A. (2000) "Learning from the Sanctions Decade", Global Policy Forum. Available at: www.globalpolicy.org/security-council/ index-of-countries-on-the-security-council-agenda/ sanctions/49076-learning-from-the-sanctions-decade.html

199. "The State of the World's Children 1996" (1996) UNICEF report. Available at: www.unicef.org/sowc96/dsanctns. htm

200. Moorcraft, Paul (1990) "Rhodesia's War of Independence", *History Today*, Volume 40, Issue 9, September

201. Biersteker, Thomas J. et al (2016) *Targeted Sanctions: The Impacts and Effectiveness of United Nations Action*, Cambridge University Press, p. 28

202. (2014) "The law of unintended consequences", Clyde and Co in association with *Commodities Now* magazine

203. (2017) "Thom Yorke Breaks Silence on Israel Controversy", *Rolling Stone*, 2nd June. Available at: https://www. rollingstone.com/music/news/thom-yorke-breaks-silence-on-israel-controversy-w485142

204. Shafak, Elif (2015) "Don't Stay Away", *The Guardian*, 2nd November

205. Bishara, Marwan (2002) *Palestine/Israel: Peace or Apartheid*, London: Zed Books, p. 121

206. Wake, Chris (2008) "An unaided peace? The (unintended) consequences of international aid on the Oslo peace process", *Conflict, Security & Development* 8:1, 109–131, DOI: 10.1080/14678800801977138

207. Andersen, Regine (2000) "How multilateral development assistance triggered the conflict in Rwanda", *Third World Quarterly* 21 (3), pp. 441–456

208. Rodrik, Dani (2006) "Goodbye Washington Consensus, Hello Washington Confusion?", Harvard University

209. Glennie, Jonathan (2008) *The Trouble with Aid: Why Less Could Mean More For Africa*, Zed Books, p. 39

210. Mutume, Gumisai (2006) "Loss of textile market costs African jobs", *Africa Renewal*, April

211. Linden, Jackie (2016) "Ghana restricts poultry meat imports", 22nd February. Available at: http://www. wattagnet.com/articles/26000-ghana-restricts-poultry-

meat-imports

212. Glennie, Jonathan (2008) *The Trouble with Aid: Why Less Could Mean More For Africa*, Zed Books, p. 54

213. Woo, Wing Thye (2004) "Serious Inadequacies of the Washington Consensus: Misunderstanding the Poor by the Brightest". From: *Diversity in Development: Reconsidering the Washington Consensus*, FONDAD, The Hague, December. Available at: www.fondad.org/product_books/pdf_down load/3/Fondad-Diversity-BookComplete.pdf

214. Quoted in Glennie, Jonathan (2008) *The Trouble with Aid: Why Less Could Mean More For Africa*, Zed Books, p. 38

215. Moyo, Dambisa (2009) "Why Foreign Aid Is Hurting Africa", *Wall Street Journal*, 21st March

216. Moyo, Dambisa (2009) "Why Foreign Aid is Hurting Africa", *Wall Street Journal*, 21st March

217. (2015) "Research In Malawi", Office of Education Abroad, Michigan State University, 30th April

218. Porter, Stephen (2016) "Accidental explosions: gunpowder in Tudor and Stuart London", 22nd September. Available at: https://www.historyextra.com/period/tudor/accidental-explosions-gunpowder-in-tudor-and-stuart-london/

219. (2012) "Kennall Vale Nature Reserve: Peaceful valley with an explosive secret!" Available at: https://www.cornish-mining.org.uk/sites/default/files/KV_Info_Sheet_v2.pdf

220. Quoted in Bown, Stephen R. (2005) *A Most Damnable Invention: Dynamite, Nitrates, and the Making of the Modern World*, Thomas Dunne Books, p. 175

221. Bown, Stephen R. (2005) *A Most Damnable Invention: Dynamite, Nitrates and the Making of the Modern World*, Thomas Dunne Books, p. 176

222. Bown, Stephen R. (2005) *A Most Damnable Invention: Dynamite, Nitrates and the Making of the Modern World*, Thomas Dunne Books, p. 176

223. Juniper, Tony (2014) "How to really stop flooding", *The*

Guardian, 5ᵗʰ February

224. Carrington, Damian (2016) "£500,000 tree-planting project helped Yorkshire town miss winter floods", *The Guardian*, 13ᵗʰ April

225. Lean, Geoffrey (2016) "UK flooding: How a Yorkshire town worked with nature to stay dry", *The Independent*, 2ⁿᵈ January

226. (2016) "Our Acquisition Of Thorneythwaite Farm", National Trust, 1ˢᵗ September. Available at: https://www.nationaltrust.org.uk/news/our-acquisition-of-thorneythwaite-farm

227. (2018) Commonwealth of Australia. Available at: http://www.environment.gov.au/biodiversity/invasive/weeds/weeds/why/impact.html

228. Pitcairn, Michael (n.d.), research scientist at the Californian Department of Food and Agriculture, quoted by DeLong, Brad (2002) "The Dreaded Yellow Star Thistle", 20ᵗʰ July. Available at: http://www.j-bradford-delong.net/movable_type/2003_archives/000638.html

229. Pimentel, David et al (2004) "Update on the environmental and economic costs associated with alien-invasive species in the United States", 29ᵗʰ December, p. 3

230. (2017) "Impacts of Invasive Species", The Nature Conservancy

231. Pimentel, David et al (2004) "Update on the environmental and economic costs associated with alien-invasive species in the United States", 29ᵗʰ December, p. 2

232. (2014) "History of grey squirrels in UK", *Daily Telegraph*, 18ᵗʰ March

233. Gilani, Nadia (2012) *Metro*, p. 19, 29ᵗʰ October

234. From Whitlock, Craig (2007) "From Nazi Past, a Proliferating Pest", *Washington Post Foreign Service*, 26ᵗʰ May

235. (n.d.) "The history of sleeping sickness", World Health Organization. Available at: http://www.who.int/

trypanosomiasis_african/country/history/en/index7.html

236. McDonald, Coby (2016) "Scientists Finally Recognized For Eradicating The Sexy Screwworm", *Popular Science*, 22nd June. Available at: https://www.popsci.com/scientists-finally-recognized-for-sexy-screwworm-research

237. Pimentel, David et al (2004) "Update on the environmental and economic costs associated with alien-invasive species in the United States", 29th December, p. 4

238. (2010) "The cane toad (Bufo marinus)", Australian Department of the Environment, Water, Heritage and the Arts

239. Bergstrom, Dana M. et al (2009) "Indirect effects of invasive species removal devastate World Heritage Island", *Journal of Applied Ecology*, Vol. 46, Issue 1, 14th January

240. (2014) "Macquarie Island: from rabbits and rodents to recovery and renewal", Australian Government, Department of the Environment. Available at: www.environment.gov.au

241. Vann, Michael G. (2003) "Of Rats, Rice and Race: The Great Hanoi Rat Massacre, an Episode in French Colonial History", *French Colonial History* 4:191–203

242. Dubner, Stephen J. and Levitt, Steven (2012) "The Cobra Effect", Freakonomics podcast, 11th October. Available at: freakonomics.com/podcast/the-cobra-effect-a-new-freakonomics-radio-podcast/

243. Rosemeyer, Joe (2017) "How Martha, Cincinnati's celebrity passenger pigeon, shaped conservation in America", 17th April. Available at: https://www.wcpo.com/news/insider/martha-cincinnatis-passenger-pigeon-reshaped-conservation-in-america

244. Housein, John Gabriel (2002) "Endangered Species and Safe Harbor Agreements: How Should They Be Used?", 24th April

245. (1996) "Developer's Guide to Endangered Species

Regulation", National Association of Home Builders

246. Dubner, Stephen J. and Levitt, Steven (2008) "Unintended Consequences", *New York Times*, 20th January

247. Kishida, Darcy (2001) "Safe Harbor Agreements Under the Endangered Species Act: Are They Right for Hawai'i?". Available at: www.hawaii.edu/elp/publications/moolelo/ ELP-PS-Summer2001.pdf

248. Peltzman, Sam (2004) "Regulation and the Natural Progress of Opulence", AEI-Brookings, Joint Center 2004 Distinguished Lecture, 8th September

249. List, John; Margolis, Michael and Osgood, Daniel, quoted in Dubner, Stephen J. and Levitt, Steven (2008) "Unintended Consequences", *New York Times*, 20th January

250. Shiffer, James Eli (1999) "Landowners Saw Opportunity in Government's Delay", *News & Observer* (Raleigh, NC), 7th March, quoted in Lueck, Dean and Michael, Jeffrey A. (2003) "Preemptive Habitat Destruction under the Endangered Species Act", *The Journal of Law and Economics* 46, no. 1, April: 27–60. Available at: https://doi.org/10.1086/344670

251. Quoted in List, John A. et al (2006) "Is the Endangered Species Act Endangering Species?", NBER Working Paper No. 12777, December, JEL No. H23,H41,Q27

252. Kishida, Darcy (2001) "Safe Harbor Agreements Under the Endangered Species Act: Are They Right for Hawai'i?". Available at: www.hawaii.edu/elp/publications/moolelo/ ELP-PS-Summer2001.pdf

253. Wilcove, D. and J. Lee (2004) "Using Economic and Regulatory Incentives to Restore Endangered Species: Lessons Learned from Three New Programs", *Conservation Biology* 18:3, pp. 639–645

254. Brown, Tim (2014) "In the developing world, a little smart thinking is leading to products that are changing the lives of millions", *Wired UK*, January, p. 144

255. Borland, Ralph (2011) "Radical Plumbers and *PlayPumps* –

Objects in development". Quoted in "10 problems with the PlayPump", objectsindevelopment.net

256. Bryson, Bill (2010) *At Home*, Doubleday, pp. 555–559

257. Suggested by Butterly, Patrick (2017) letter to *The Guardian*, 6th May

258. (2016) "Statistics On Smoking", Health and Social Care Information Centre, 27th May

259. (2014) "The Health Consequences of Smoking – 50 Years of Progress: A Report of the Surgeon General. Atlanta", US Department of Health and Human Services

260. (2017) "Tobacco", WHO factsheet, May

261. Wangdi, Kencho (2011) "Do Bhutan's Anti-Smoking Laws Go Too Far?", *Time*, 12th April

262. According to HMRC (customs element) and the Tobacco Manufacturers' Association (VAT element)

263. Allender, S. et al (2009) "The burden of smoking-related ill health in the United Kingdom", Department of Public Health, University of Oxford, Oxford, UK

264. (2014) "Tobacco Levy: Consultation", HM Treasury, December

265. Crawford, Angus (2016) "The town in Belarus from where cigarettes are smuggled to the UK", *BBC News*, 1st December. Available at: http://www.bbc.co.uk/news/uk-38170754

266. Boseley, Sarah (2017) "Smoking numbers hit new low as Britons turn to vaping to help quit cigarettes", *The Guardian*, 7th March

267. (2007) US Tar, Nicotine, and Carbon Monoxide Report

268. Harris, Bradford (2011) "The intractable cigarette 'filter problem'", BMJ Publishing Group Limited, 10.1136/tc.2010.040113

269. Harris, Bradford (2011) "The intractable cigarette 'filter problem'", BMJ Publishing Group Limited, 10.1136/tc.2010.040113

270. (2001) "What does the filter on a cigarette do?", HowStuffWorks.com, 4th June. Available at: https://science.howstuffworks.com/innovation/science-questions/question650.htm

271. Warner, Kenneth E. and Slade, John (1992) "Low Tar, High Toll", *American Journal of Public Health*, vol. 82, no. 1 (January), pp. 17–18, quoted in Tenner, Edward (1996) *Why Things Bite Back*, Random House Inc., p. 82

272. Brown, Adam Tod (2009) "5 Idiotic Health Campaigns That Backfired (Hilariously)", 9th April. Available at: http://www.cracked.com/article_17224_5-retarded-health-campaigns-that-backfired-hilariously.html

273. (2016) "Obesity", NHS Choices, 15th June. Available at: http://www.nhs.uk/conditions/Obesity/Pages/Introduction.aspx

274. Major, Brenda et al (2014) "The ironic effects of weight stigma", *Journal of Experimental Social Psychology*, Volume 51, March, pp. 74–80

275. Burkeman, Oliver (2013) "From weight loss to fundraising, 'ironic effects' can sabotage our best-laid plans", Oliver Burkeman's Blog, *The Guardian*, 12th December

276. Chiou, W.-B. et al (2011) "A randomized experiment to examine unintended consequences of dietary supplement use among daily smokers: taking supplements reduces self-regulation of smoking", *Addiction* 106: pp. 2221–2228, doi:10.1111/j.1360-0443.2011.03545.x

277. Provencher, Véronique et al (2008) "Perceived healthiness of food. If it's healthy, you can eat more!", Department of Psychology, University of Toronto, Canada, 14th November

278. Morris, Steven (2016) "Activists say badger cull has increased bovine TB", *The Guardian*, 20th February

279. (2016) Bovine TB Statistics, Animal and Plant Health Agency figures, 15th May

280. (2016) Bovine TB Statistics, Animal and Plant Health Agency figures, 15th May

281. McLean, Ross (2016) "Bomb gaffe KO's United game", *City A.M.*, 16th May

282. Hiltzik, Michael (2016) "50 years after we 'almost lost Detroit,' America's nuclear power industry faces even graver doubts", *Los Angeles Times*, 3rd October. Available at: www.latimes.com/business/hiltzik/la-fi-hiltzik-detroit-nuclear-20161003-snap-story.html

283. Lochbaum, David (2016) "Nuclear Plant Accidents: Fermi Unit 1", 12th July. Available at: http://allthingsnuclear.org/dlochbaum/nuclear-plant-accidents-fermi-unit-1

284. Bird, David (1982) "Operator At 3 Mile Island Asserts Safety Training Was Inadequate", *New York Times*, 7th December

285. Harford, Tim (2011) "What we can learn from a nuclear reactor", *Financial Times*, 14th January

286. (2015) "Reported Road Casualties Great Britain: 2014", Department for Transport, September

287. Vernon, HM (1941) "Road-deaths in War-time", *The Spectator*, 10th October

288. Streff, FM and Geller, ES (1988) "An experimental test of risk compensation: Between-subject versus within-subject analyses", *Accident Analysis and Prevention* 20 (4): August, pp. 277–87

289. Janssen, W. (1994) "Seat-belt wearing and driving behavior: An instrumented-vehicle study", *Accident Analysis and Prevention* 26, pp. 249–261

290. (2015) "Reported Road Casualties Great Britain: 2014", Department for Transport, September

291. (2003) *The Scotsman*, 8th February

292. Jenkins, Simon (2012) *London Evening Standard*, 7th February

293. Austin, Henry (2016) "Road Markings: Removing white lines may cause motorists to slow down, research finds", *The Independent*, 3rd February

294. Akwagyiram, Alexis (2005) "Can 'naked roads' kill speed?", *BBC News*, 31st January. Available at: http://news.

bbc.co.uk/1/hi/magazine/4213221.stm

295. Rudlin, David (2010) "New Road – Brighton", The Academy of Urbanism, August. Available at: https://www.academyofurbanism.org.uk/new-road/

296. Rudlin, David (2010) "New Road – Brighton", The Academy of Urbanism, August. Available at: https://www.academyofurbanism.org.uk/new-road/

297. (2016) "Shared Space – reducing the dominance of motor vehicles", The Landmark Practice, 6th April. Available at: https://thelandmarkpractice.com/shared-space-reducing-dominance-motor-vehicles/

298. Petersen, Jim (1994-95) "The 1910 Fire", Evergreen Magazine, Winter Edition

299. (n.d.) "The 1910 Fires", The Forest Historical Society. Available at: https://foresthistory.org/research-explore/us-forest-service-history/policy-and-law/fire-u-s-forest-service/famous-fires/the-1910-fires/

300. (2001) "Review and Update of the 1995 Federal Wildland Fire Management Policy", US National Interagency Fire Center, January

301. Gabbert, Bill (2015) "New normal; more megafires", Wildfire Today. Available at: https://wildfiretoday.com/2015/05/05/new-normal--more-megafires-per-year/

302. Diamond, Jared (2005) Collapse: How Societies Choose to Fail or Succeed, Penguin Books, p. 44

303. Both quoted in Mathiesen, Karl (2016) "How forest management helps lay the conditions for wildfires", The Guardian, 6th May

304. Bleiker, Carla (2016) "Martell: 'Fire is a natural part of forest ecosystems in Canada'", dw.com, 10th May. Available at: http://www.dw.com/en/martell-fire-is-a-natural-part-of-forest-ecosystems-in-canada/a-19247762

305. Augustin, Kizzy and Brooks, Oliver (2015) "The effectiveness of the Health and Safety at Work Act", Safety

and Health Practitioner, 14th September. Available at: https://www.shponline.co.uk/an-analysis-of-the-effectiveness-of-the-health-and-safety-at-work-act/

306. Pemberton, Dr Max (2015) "How to stop smoking by talking", *Daily Telegraph*, 20th January; and (2014) "Want to quit smoking?", *Daily Mail*, 28th December

307. Sitwell, William (2016) *Eggs or Anarchy: The Remarkable Story of the Man Tasked with the Impossible: To Feed a Nation at War*, Simon & Schuster, p. 56

308. Sitwell, William (2016) *Eggs or Anarchy: The Remarkable Story of the Man Tasked with the Impossible: To Feed a Nation at War*, Simon & Schuster, p. 56

309. (2002) "The health of the nation was surprisingly good at the time, despite the physical and emotional stresses." What was life like in the Second World War? What did they eat? © Imperial War Museum

310. Sitwell, William (2016) *Eggs or Anarchy: The Remarkable Story of the Man Tasked with the Impossible: To Feed a Nation at War*, Simon & Schuster, pp. 81, 305

311. Atkinson, Louise (2007) "Can a modern family survive on wartime rations?", *Daily Mail*, 2nd July

312. Ruhm, Christopher J. (2015) "Health Effects Of Economic Crises", Working Paper 21604, October. Available at: http://www.nber.org/papers/w21604

313. Weyer, Christian et al (2000) "Energy metabolism after 2 y of energy restriction: the Biosphere 2 experiment", *American Journal of Clinical Nutrition*, Volume 72, No. 4, 946–953, October

314. (2014) "London Tube strike coverage", *BBC News*, 5th February. Available at: http://www.bbc.co.uk/news/uk-england-london-26037534

315. Lynch, Russell (2015) "Listen to the wonks: it pays to shake things up sometimes", *London Evening Standard*, 17th September

316. (2013) "The State of Food and Agriculture 2013", United Nations Food and Agricultural Organization

317. Tertullian (197) *Apologeticus*, Chapter 50

318. Anwar, Harris (2013) "Taliban intimidation backfires as shot teenager inspires school enrollment surge", *Bloomberg News*, 13th October. Available at: https://www. registercitizen.com/news/article/Taliban-intimidation-backfires-as-shot-teenager-12018363.php

319. Yousafzai, Malala (2014) *Malala: The Girl Who Stood Up for Education and Changed the World*, Orion Books

320. Roberts, Justine (2015) "Mumsnet is really my other baby", Justine Roberts, *The Guardian*, 21st March

321. Jeffries, Stuart (2014) "Water, super-sewers and the filth threatening the River Thames", *The Guardian*, 22nd July

322. Lemon, Johanna (2018) "The Great Stink", Cholera and the Thames. Available at: http://www.choleraandthethames. co.uk/cholera-in-london/the-great-stink

323. Halpern, David (2016) *Inside the Nudge Unit*, WH Allen, pp. 66–69

324. Halpern, David (2016) *Inside the Nudge Unit*, WH Allen, pp. 66–69

325. (2018) "Suicide Statistics", American Foundation For Suicide Prevention. Available at: https://afsp.org/about-suicide/suicide-statistics/

326. Roberts, Royston M. (1989) *Serendipity*, John Wiley & Sons, p. ix

327. Comroe, Julius H. (1977) *Retrospectroscope: Insights into Medical Discovery*, Von Gehr

328. Roberts, Royston M. (1989) *Serendipity*, John Wiley & Sons, pp. 187–189

329. Andrews, Evan (2015) "Why is purple considered the color of royalty?", History.com, 15th July. Available at: http://www.history.com/news/ask-history/why-is-purple-considered-the-color-of-royalty

330. (2006) "Sir William Henry Perkin (1838–1907); the Discovery of Aniline Purple", the Museum of Science and Industry in Manchester

331. Donnelly, Tim (2012) "9 Brilliant Inventions Made by Mistake", Inc.com, 23rd August. Available at: https://www.inc.com/tim-donnelly/brilliant-failures/9-inventions-made-by-mistake.html

332. Williamson, Marcus (2011) "Wilson Greatbatch: Inventor of the implantable cardiac pacemaker", Obituary, *The Independent*, 30th September

333. Hart, GJ (2003) "Science sometimes has unintended consequences", the *Exchange* 10(2):6,7

334. Roberts, Royston M. (1989) *Serendipity*, John Wiley & Sons, pp. 220–221

335. (2006) "Neil Armstrong's Flown Suit", NASA. Available at: https://www.hq.nasa.gov/alsj/a11/A11NAAFlownSuit.html

336. (2007) "Working on the Moon". Available at: http://www.workingonthemoon.com/WOTM-Velcro.html

337. Chesto, Jon (2015) "Velcro: Not your father's fastener", *Boston Globe*, 1st December

338. Proverbs 14:12, King James Bible (Cambridge Edition)

339. Thompson, Dr George (2005) "7 things never to say to anyone, and why", 11th November. Available at: http://policeone.com/communications/articles/120708

340. DiJulio, Bianca et al (2015) "Data Note: Americans' Views On The U.S. Role In Global Health", Henry J. Kaiser Family Foundation, 23rd January. Available at: https://www.kff.org/global-health-policy/poll-finding/data-note-americans-views-on-the-u-s-role-in-global-health

341. Ariely, Dan (2015) "The Ordeal That Made Me a Student of Humanity", *Wall Street Journal*, 30th July

342. (2018) "Good News". Available at: https://www.climateoptimist.org/good-news/

343. (2017) "85% of Germany's power just came from renewable energy, setting a new record", Indy100. Available at: https://www.indy100.com/article/two-thirds-germany-powered-renewable-energy-easter-day-green-7737221

344. (2018) "Carbon dioxide emissions from energy consumption in the U.S. from 1975 and 2017 (in million metric tons of carbon dioxide)". Available at: https://www.statista.com/statistics/183943/us-carbon-dioxide-emissions-from-1999/

345. Herrmann, Victoria (2017) "Doomsday narratives about climate change don't work. But here's what does", *The Guardian*, 12th July

346. Balmford, Andrew and Knowlton, Nancy (2017) "Why Earth Optimism", *Science* 356 (6335), 225, 20th April, doi: 10.1126/science.aan4082

347. (n.d.) "Check your tire pressure, reduce pollution", Minnesota Pollution Control Agency. Available at: https://www.pca.state.mn.us/living-green/check-your-tire-pressure-reduce-pollution

348. (2016) The Behavioural Insights Team – Update Report 2015-16

349. Burkeman, Oliver (2015) "If everyone's at it, how bad can it be?", *The Guardian*, 23rd May

350. Campbell, Melissa, ed. (2014) "#DoodleUs: Gender & Race in Google Doodles", SPARK Movement. Available at: http://www.sparkmovement.org/wp-content/uploads/2014/02/doodle-research-summary-2.pdf

351. Silva, Rohan (2015) "Celebrating women in technology is the way to attract more", *London Evening Standard*, 17th August

352. Pascal, Blaise (1654) *Pensées*

353. Bliss, MD, Garrison (2017) "The Benefit of Doing Nothing in Healthcare", 7th May. Available at: https://thedoctorweighsin.com/the-benefit-of-doing-nothing-in-healthcare/

354. Kale, MS et al (2011) "'Top 5' Lists Top $5 Billion", *Arch Intern Med.*, 2011;171(20):1858–1859. doi:10.1001/archinternmed.2011.501

355. Cunningham, Solveig Argeseanu (2008) "Doctors' strikes and mortality: A review", *Social Science & Medicine* 67, pp. 1784–1788

356. Collinson, Patrick (2018) "Is Terry Smith the best money manager Britain has ever had?", *The Guardian*, 8th September

357. Mitchell, Andrew, MP (2010) *"War Games: the Story of Aid and War in Modern Times* by Linda Polman: review", *Daily Telegraph*, 7th May

358. Quoted in Rifkind, Hugo (2012) "For a genius drugs policy, look to California", *The Times*, 16th October

359. Butler, Patrick (2016) the Saturday interview with Sharon Shoesmith, *The Guardian*, 20th August

Acknowledgements

Thanks once more to Dixe Wills for his unflagging enthusiasm and wise advice and to many other family and friends for their help and encouragement over this book's (somewhat lengthy) gestation. Shaena, Edwin, Ptolemy and Olivia Wills and Hazel and Geoff Wills all deserve special mentions, as does Ben Mason for his support. Thanks also to Les Blythe for his excellent Economics lessons in the dim and distant past, as well as to Professor Sir Richard Sorabji and Stephen Navin for being generally inspiring in years gone by and to Professor Steven Gunn, who made it look as though writing a book could be rather fun. A shout-out too to Southern Rail, on whose (oft-delayed) trains much of this book was written. And to any who I have (unintendedly) omitted, my apologies.

Acknowledgements

Iff Books

ACADEMIC AND SPECIALIST

Iff Books publishes non-fiction. It aims to work with authors and titles that augment our understanding of the human condition, society and civilisation, and the world or universe in which we live.
If you have enjoyed this book, why not tell other readers by posting a review on your preferred book site.

Recent bestsellers from Iff Books are:

Why Materialism Is Baloney
How true skeptics know there is no death and fathom answers to
life, the universe, and everything
Bernardo Kastrup
A hard-nosed, logical, and skeptic non-materialist metaphysics,
according to which the body is in mind, not mind in the body.
Paperback: 978-1-78279-362-5 ebook: 978-1-78279-361-8

The Fall
Steve Taylor
The Fall discusses human achievement versus the issues of war,
patriarchy and social inequality.
Paperback: 978-1-78535-804-3 ebook:978-1-78535-805-0

Brief Peeks Beyond
Critical essays on metaphysics, neuroscience, free will, skepticism
and culture
Bernardo Kastrup
An incisive, original, compelling alternative to current mainstream
cultural views and assumptions.
Paperback: 978-1-78535-018-4 ebook: 978-1-78535-019-1

Framespotting
Changing how you look at things changes how you see them
Laurence & Alison Matthews
A punchy, upbeat guide to framespotting. Spot deceptions and
hidden assumptions; swap growth for growing up. See and be free.
Paperback: 978-1-78279-689-3 ebook: 978-1-78279-822-4

Is There an Afterlife?
David Fontana

Is there an Afterlife? If so what is it like? How do Western ideas
of the afterlife compare with Eastern? David Fontana presents
the historical and contemporary evidence for survival of physical
death.
Paperback: 978-1-90381-690-5

Nothing Matters
a book about nothing
Ronald Green

Thinking about Nothing opens the world to everything by
illuminating new angles to old problems and stimulating new
ways of thinking.
Paperback: 978-1-84694-707-0 ebook: 978-1-78099-016-3

Panpsychism
The Philosophy of the Sensuous Cosmos
Peter Ells

Are free will and mind chimeras? This book, anti-materialistic
but respecting science, answers: No! Mind is foundational to all
existence.
Paperback: 978-1-84694-505-2 ebook: 978-1-78099-018-7

Punk Science
Inside the Mind of God
Manjir Samanta-Laughton

Many have experienced unexplainable phenomena; God, psychic
abilities, extraordinary healing and angelic encounters. Can
cutting-edge science actually explain phenomena
previously thought of as 'paranormal'?
Paperback: 978-1-90504-793-2

The Vagabond Spirit of Poetry
Edward Clarke
Spend time with the wisest poets of the modern age and of the past, and let Edward Clarke remind you of the importance of poetry in our industrialized world.
Paperback: 978-1-78279-370-0 ebook: 978-1-78279-369-4

Readers of ebooks can buy or view any of these bestsellers by clicking on the live link in the title. Most titles are published in paperback and as an ebook. Paperbacks are available in traditional bookshops. Both print and ebook formats are available online.

Find more titles and sign up to our readers' newsletter at
http://www.johnhuntpublishing.com/non-fiction

Follow us on Facebook at
https://www.facebook.com/JHPNonFiction
and Twitter at
https://twitter.com/JHPNonFiction

Acknowledgements